THE
LITTLE FOXES

Things Christians do <u>not</u> have to do

By

Bertist Rouse

First published by AuthorHouse 04/07/04

ISBN: 1-4184-0927-8 (e-book)
ISBN: 1-4184-0928-6 (Paperback)
ISBN: 1-4184-0929-4 (Dust Jacket)

Printed in the United States of America
Bloomington, Indiana

This book is printed on acid-free paper.

Unless otherwise noted, all scripture references in this book are from the Authorized King James Version of 1611. Other versions referred to herein are as follows:

— The Amplified Version (Amp.) —
— The New American Standard Version (NASB) —
— The New International Version (NIV) —
— The New English Bible (NEB) —
— The New Testament in Modern English, by J. B. Phillips (Phillips) —
— The Today's English Version (TEV) —

About the Author...
Bertist C. Rouse
November 2, 1936 – November 18, 2003

Dr. Bertist Rouse is the Founder and President of International Gospel Outreach (IGO), an interdenominational missions agency based in Semmes, Alabama. IGO is a servant ministry, with missionary work in many nations of the world, as well as ministry at home in the United States. With over 43 years experience as a pastor, evangelist and missionary, Bertist is uniquely qualified to address the issues of the 'little weights' in our lives that burden us down and hinder our Christian witness.

This is the fourth printing of the book "The Little Foxes" and is dedicated in loving memory of his life and work in the Gospel.

Acknowledgements

For the final publication of this book I am deeply indebted to my lovely wife, Anna Merle and to our entire office staff. These lovely people, who keep International Gospel Outreach moving, have been such a tremendous help to me during the time consuming months of the writing of this little volume. They have helped beyond my ability to thank them and show my appreciation for their contributions.

Thanksgiving is also in order for their willingness to encourage me in the over-all process of seeing it come to completion. They are to be commended for helping me with proof-reading and editing and have bravely pointed out my errors and mistakes. This group of brave soldiers of the cross have also helped in giving me some much needed training in word processing and typesetting. Amazingly, they have patiently stayed with me during this entire venture. They truly know what the Lord meant when He said, *"He that endureth to the end shall be saved."*

Dedication

It is with great pleasure and humility that I dedicate this work to my wife and eternal sweetheart, Anna Merle, who has been a sounding board and monitor for all the positive things I have used as a standard for the writing of this book. She has unwittingly co-authored this book by her constant high standard of holiness and sobriety across the years of our lives and ministry together.

Also, to my parents, Coleman and Orell Rouse, who, from the very beginning, taught me the difference between right and wrong. And to my children who gave me ample opportunity to try to live a righteous life and teach them to do the same.

Then, to my fellow Christians, who, because of their continued Christian witness have encouraged and reminded me to be accountable to them and to our Lord concerning Godliness. I haven't always been where I desired to be in my walk with Jesus, but these people have renewed my thinking and shaken my conscience as to where I needed to be.

Contents

"It Is The Little Foxes That Spoil The Vines"

In this discourse we are not addressing gross sin. The targets are not murder, morals, or money. Those we zoom in on are more difficult to ascertain, yet their presence occupy most of our hearts and minds. We are looking at certain things the enemy uses to 'beset us,' by dulling our plowshares and pruning hooks, as well as our battle axes. Solomon, in his *'Song of Songs'*, makes reference to something that brings our subject matter into a little sharper focus.

"Catch the foxes for us, the little foxes that are ruining the vineyards, while our vineyards are in blossom." (Song of Solomon 2:15, NASB)

The analogy here is a reference to Solomon's love for the Shulammite maiden and is to be used to show God's love for Israel and Christ's love for His Bride, the Church. "Foxes" in scripture are types of:

Enemies of the Church (Song of Solomon 2:15).

False prophets (Ezekiel 13:4). "Israel, thy prophets are like the foxes in the desert."

Desolation (Lamentations 5:18). "Because of the mountain of Zion, which is desolate, the foxes walk upon it."

Craftiness (Luke 13:32). Because of King Herod's deceptive and shrewd manipulation, Jesus called him a fox. Herod was indeed sly, cowardly and cunning.

The Wycliffe Bible Commentary also says of the passage from The Song of Solomon, "These are the bride's own words. **The foxes, are likely the annoyances and cares that may interfere with and damage their love. Their love is fully blossoming, and nothing should be allowed to disturb it."**[1]

What about your love and intimacy with Jesus? Is there continually a wedge being driven between you and your Savior because of many little things? In this discourse we will expose some of the foxes that are sapping your strength. We leave it up to you to catch and evict them, as best you can, from your spirit, soul, and body (I Thessalonians 5:23).

These Foxes Can Set Your Fields on Fire

Let me add this admonition concerning foxes. Not only can these little foxes abort your fruit in its blossoming stages, but can set your fields on fire as in Judges 15:4 & 5. Samson, in his bitter rage of revenge against the Philistines, took 300 foxes, tied each one's tail to another, put a lighted torch on each pair of tails and turned them loose in the 'ready-for-harvest' wheat fields. It destroyed the entire crop. These foxes can abort certain things in their infant stages of your life and walk with Jesus or they can exterminate it before harvest.

Purge Yourself

You will find as you make this study that these little foxes are the works of the flesh and the works of the devil and truly need to be dealt with personally. Be sure to do so and rid yourself of all the excess baggage that the devil laid on you by these little foxes that spoil your character, your effectiveness, and your fellowship with Jesus. Please keep in mind the following scripture as you pursue this study.

> ***"..All that is in the world-the lust of the flesh* [craving for sensual gratification] *and the lust of the eyes* [greedy longings of the mind] *and the pride of life* [assurance in one's own resources or in the stability of earthly things]- THESE DO NOT COME FROM THE FATHER BUT ARE FROM THE WORLD* [ITSELF]. *And the world passes away and disappears, and with it the forbidden cravings* (the passionate desires, the lust) *of it; but he who does the will of God and carries out His purposes in his life abides* (remains) *forever." (I John 2:16 & 17 Amp.)***

Obedience is the Best Policy

We are attempting to inform the Christian that he does not have to do the things we have listed. We need to catch the foxes that spoil (KJV), i.e., "pervert, destroy, deal corruptly" (Strong's Exhaustive Concordance) with the fruit of our labors Why? Because "our vines have tender grapes." And if we do not catch the foxes they will, through us, prevent an abundant harvest, as well as cause us to cast forth the wrong image of ourselves and of God. Why not be obedient to the Word of God and *"catch the foxes, ... The little foxes, that are ruining the vineyards"?*

Demonic or in the Flesh?

Some of the things that we address as excess baggage, and are needlessly straining and draining our spiritual stockpile, are demonic. And, if so, they can be cast out in the Name and Authority of Jesus. But other pieces of this unnecessary luggage are of the flesh. These cannot be cast out. To rid ourselves of these weights that 'so easily beset us' calls for a crucifixion of the flesh. It demands a great deal of special, strenuous application on our part. If it is a demon it is much easier, especially if we truly desire to rid ourselves of it. But if it is the flesh, it is not so easy. It will require an extreme portion of grit, grace and sincere fasting and praying.

As you read, study and meditate on the material in this volume, you will find from one chapter to another, **some duplications and some repetition. They were put there by both purpose and providence.** Purpose, because we are targeting the situation being dealt with. Providence, because God desires to emphasize something. You may also, as you continue to move through this treatise, think that some of it is extremely elementary, and you will be correct in your judgment. But that is the purpose of the entire venture. Too many people in the church have never been challenged nor informed about sin, its dangers, its degrading influences, and its worthlessness in the life of a Christian. They haven't been made aware that they do not have to yield to its pressures nor surrender to any of its enchantment.

Bertist Rouse, Mobile, Alabama, January, 1994

Foreword 1994

Many books have come and gone concerning **Holiness** from a Wesleyan/Armenian persuasion. Here is another one. So who needs it? *We do!*

In a culture based on personal freedom and civil rights, we are well acquainted with all the privileges, but still struggle with the responsibilities of living the Christian faith in a post-Christian nation.

In this book, Bertist Rouse addresses some of the forgotten rights we have as Christian disciples. We have been trained to think in terms of our 'inalienable right', from the time we first read of early American history. But this book speaks to the awesome privilege we have, as Citizens of the Kingdom of God, to not conform to standards of behavior propagated by the world around us. We possess a freedom of choice to live according to higher, holier ethic.

In a day when the moral foundations of our world are teetering, pivoting away from the ethical standard of God's Word, it is indeed refreshing to hear a voice crying out in the wilderness.

So prepare ye the way for the Lord to speak to you in the midst of this little book. May you live by all your rights as a Child of the Lord Almighty.

David Fackler,
Administrator
International Gospel Outreach Mobile, Alabama
March 1994

Forward 2003

Reading this book will shine a light on the problems in our own lives, as well as on the local church, corporately. There are twenty areas addressed in this book that we, as Christians, do not have to do.

As we read through the book's contents, we find ourselves caught up in one or more of these areas. The truths found in Little Foxes will really hit home, if we will allow them to penetrate the depths of our soul. It will cause us to take serious stock in our own lives.

The age we live in today does not seem to have a solid moral foundation. We hear more about "rights" than we do about responsibility and accountability. It is true that we have rights, but as Dr. Rouse states, "When we exercise our rights, we are usually stepping on the rights of others."

God, through Little Foxes, will cause the flaws and the dross in our lives to come to the surface, so it can be removed if we will let it. It will help us get rid of the "excess baggage" that the devil has us carrying around.

Prepare for an adventure while reading this book. You will not be able to put it down until you have read it through. Even though Little Foxes addresses serious issues, you will fine much humor in this book. You will find yourself laughing, crying, examining your issues, examining your motives, literally examining all, confessing and repenting.

Listen to your inner man and allow the Lord to speak to you as you read this book.

Dr. Verda Thompson
American Mission Teams President
International College of Bible Theology
Norris City, Illinois
October 2003

Introduction

The Little Foxes
Things Christians Do Not Have To Do

In this book you are not going to read, as it were, the headlines exposing the latest news about a televangelist who has forfeited his 'exciting' ministry because of money, murder, or morals. This entire discourse deals with things that seem to be petty and insignificant. Nevertheless, they are present and need to be eradicated from the attitude and conduct of our lives. These 'little foxes' are unwarranted, unfruitful, unnecessary, and unbecoming in our walk with Jesus. Besides, any compromise with these little foxes starts us on the road to destruction. To the Christian who truly desires to live a life of holiness before God, there are no little sins or big sins. All sin is sin. There is absolutely no place in the Christian life for them. The things we are not compelled to do are those extra weights and sins that restrict the progressive growth and spiritual expression of our lives.

"Wherefore, seeing we are compassed about with so great a cloud of witnesses, let us lay aside every weight, and the sin which doth so easily beset us, and let us run with patience the race that is set before us." (Hebrews 12:1)

The word *"eradicate"* comes from the Latin, "E" (out), plus "RADIX" (root), hence: "to pull out by the roots" (Reader's Digest Thesaurus).[2] An elementary definition of the word: *"eradicate"* from Webster's New World Dictionary is *"to uproot and move completely; get rid of; wipe out." Our proposition in this study is to challenge Christians to 'get rid of' those little sins that "so easily beset" them, those little foxes that spoil the vines and abort the harvest.* Or as another version states it: the *"sins that entangle us."* Many Christians need to get "untangled" from the web that Satan has so cunningly charmed them into. He has done so by shrewdly manipulating them into being distributors of his ungodly merchandise.

Parasitic Merchandise

There are certain items of merchandise in your spiritual warehouse that have no significant, spiritual reason for being there. They were placed there by the enemy to stunt your spiritual growth and render you helpless in spiritual warfare, and cause you to be a drawback to others. They also stand in the way of your being in a position to help others in coming to Christ, as well as hindering you in helping Christians in their walk with Christ. In most other cases, these excess commodities actually cause you to work for the enemy.

Taxation Without Compensation

With all this excess baggage, you are taxed beyond your limit to really make a profitable and lasting spiritual contribution in bringing honor to Christ and building His Kingdom on earth. Think about it, you have to pay extra for having this spiritual vampire bleeding you down and rendering you helpless in the cause of Christ. You have to pay transportation costs for conveying it. You have to book-keep it and maintain it. You must feed it. You have to pay storage fees on it. Because of the drain it puts on your spiritual reserve, you have to pay 'late-charges' or late fees on your good, spiritual responsibilities. Why? Because you wasted your time and your investment trying to satisfy your 'primary obligation' of being a good steward over the devil's resources. In some cases you pay nothing on your honest, spiritual dues and duties because you spent all your energy maintaining Satan's assets. Yes, Satan will tax you heavily for working for him, but he will not compensate you for it. What it boils down to is this, you pay him to get to work for him.

Time For A Warehouse Extermination

Hey man, wake up! Doesn't it make good common and spiritual sense to get rid of the Devil's unprofitable possessions that you have to maintain. Really and truly, you DO NOT have to keep this stuff. Nowhere in the Bible does God tell you that you must hang on to this kind of baggage. If you hang on to this unnecessary "junk," you are actually stealing from the treasury of Heaven and misappropriating funds (spiritual) God had already allocated or 'ear-marked' for kingdom advancement. So, the smart thing for you to do is rid yourself of this trash. Please remember Friend, if you don't clean up your house, God will do it for you! It would be much cheaper if you do it. God's services, in matters like this, are very expensive.

"Our Business is Picking Up"

A bumper sticker on the back of a garbage truck said, *"Our business is picking up."* As I pondered over this statement I thought, there are many people in the Body of Christ who bear the same testimony as that garbage truck. They are constantly picking up, but they are picking the wrong stuff, garbage. They feel they are under compulsion to pick the devil's garbage because they see other people picking up and carrying some of the devil's junk. Or, they are doing it because they want to be cool, like everybody else; it's the "in" thing to do. The purpose of this little book is to announce the good news that they do not have to hustle all the things listed in this book. Is your business picking up? If so, what are you picking up? If your business is picking up the devil's garbage, throw it down immediately!!

Paul's Testimony of Jesus

The Apostle Paul witnessed to the fact that Jesus did not waste His time nor sap His strength hustling the Devil's luggage. Christians should take note and learn from the Master. We are not the Devil's skycaps or bellhops. Here's how Paul explained the way in which Jesus handled the situation:

Jesus, *"Made Himself of no reputation, and took upon Him the form of a servant, and was made in the likeness of men: and being found in fashion as a man, He humbled Himself and became obedient unto death, even the death of the cross."* (Philippians 2:7, 8)

Meditate on this scripture and allow the Lord's attitude and behavior to become yours, and learn from Him how to handle situations that come your way.

The Humiliation of Christ

The entire 2nd Chapter of Paul's letter to the Philippians deals with the ideal pattern of behavior and attitude of the individual born of God. The apostle uses Christ as his exalted standard or model to give the born-again child of God guidance in living the Christ-life before the world and the church. In verse 5 he relates to us the way in which Jesus viewed the situation. And, he also challenged the church to have the same mind in the matter. In spite of His exalted position, Jesus chose to keep a low profile. That's exactly what the apostle admonishes us to do.

The attitude of Jesus is expressed in verses 5 and 6, and His behavior is shared with us in verses 7 and 9. But His character is portrayed in detail in the Gospels. The Lord's attitude and conduct should be exhibited in the heart and lives of Christian people everywhere.

Even though Jesus is rightly projected as the Exalted Lord, He chose, by the act of His own volition, to think and act as He did. Jesus chose the lowly path of humble service. If you would operate the way He did you wouldn't have to fabricate anything to conceal your unexpressed motives.

Let me speak into your life with this bit of scriptural advice and wisdom: ***Allow the same mind to "be in you which was in Christ Jesus."***

JESUS CHOSE NOT to peddle the Devil's merchandise. We have the same prerogative. ***We do not have to display nor distribute Satan's goods!*** We are free moral agents. We have the option to choose or not to choose to transport and employ the devil's cargo and services. Christians everywhere are paying an extreme and exorbitant price for maintaining the devil's merchandise, when all they would have to do is lay it down. Some people would rather climb a tall tree to tell a lie, when they could simply stand on the ground and tell the truth. *That's exactly what we are attempting to say,* ***You do not have to go to all that extra trouble and expense to do all these unnecessary things.*** Now relax and read about some things you do not have to do. Learn some simple things that will save you time, energy, embarrassment, explanation, regret, repentance and remorse. **Why don't you catch those little foxes before they spoil your vines and prevent a Godly harvest.**

Chapter 1

You Do Not

Have To Tell Everything You Know

Don't spill all your beans at any one setting. Save some for next time. Besides, many things do not need to be told anyway. Solomon said, *"A prudent man keeps his knowledge to himself, but the heart of fools blurts out folly"* (Proverbs 12:23 NIV). If it is not relevant to what God is saying or attempting to do, you could ruin the opportunity you have before you. Let someone else have the floor. Give them a chance to speak. Don't allow the Devil to have the opportunity to accuse you of being talkative or call you 'motor-mouth' or 'ratchet-jaw.' *Besides, there is a great ministry in just 'listening.'*

The "Bible" word for this type of conduct is *"prating,"* especially in the King James Version. The verb "prate" means "to talk idly and at great length; chatter. To utter idly or to little purpose. Empty, foolish and trivial talk"[3]

Check this out: *"The wise in heart will receive commandments: but a prating fool shall fall"* (Proverbs. 10:8). The NASB translates the *"prating fool"* as *"a babbling fool."*

Please meditate on the verses that follow and allow God to speak to you from them.

> *"Guard your steps as you go to the house of God, and draw near to listen rather than to offer the sacrifice of fools; Do not be hasty in word, …let your words be few. The dream comes through much effort and the voice of a fool through many words… Do not let your speech cause you to sin… For in many dreams and in many words there is emptiness."* (Ecclesiastes 5:1, 2, 3, 6 & 7 NASB)

If we get serious about the problem of 'prating' we will find that the *Holy Spirit is very serious also.* He rises up to address the situation many times in the Holy Scriptures. Evidently, He foresaw many perils and the extreme jeopardy that a prater would encounter as he rushes into life. At this juncture let me pause to remind you, that prating is a serious sin and needs to be avoided at all costs. So, position yourself to be on the alert and stand ready to defend yourself from Satan's guerrilla attacks. Let's tune in on the Holy Spirit and glean from Him more truths about the use of a long and flapping tongue. We shall also see some of the pitfalls that lie ahead for the individual who possesses an over productive tongue.

As mentioned above, *the Bible calls a prater a fool.* This will be addressed indirectly as we move through the progression of this study on an over prolific tongue. Because of its severity, *the Holy Spirit cannot keep quiet about the frequent overuse of the tongue.*

First, we need to address the severity of the frequent overuse of this little and unruly member. This kind of demeanor from human lips is assaulted very heavily in scripture. *The prater is like Judas Iscariot, and is a son of perdition (destruction).* In Proverbs, Solomon said, *"The one who guards his mouth preserves his life, the one who opens wide his mouth comes to ruin"* (13:3, NASB). The NIV calls this unfortunate person, *"The one who speaks rashly."*

Then, in Proverbs 18:7 another storm warning is announced: *"A fool's mouth is his destruction, and his lips are the snare of his soul."* It means that a fool and his tongue are on a collision course to ruin. Then, another word from Proverbs is this: *"Wise men lay up knowledge: but the mouth of the foolish is near destruction"* (10:14).

Another important factor that needs to be dealt with is that **vain talk is a seed-bed for sin and transgression.** Again, the wisdom of Solomon gives us another base from which we can work to address this curse that has plagued so many good people. *"Where there are many words, transgression is unavoidable"* (NASB), or from the Amplified, *"In a multitude of words transgression is not lacking"* (Proverbs 10:19). The more he talks, the more transgression and iniquity he dumps on himself and his listeners. When a prater begins to unload on you his empty words, stop it or flee from it! You do not need to allow this kind of evil spirit to enter your re-created human spirit.

Talking too much leads to poverty. *"In all labor there is profit but the talk of the lips tendeth only to penury"* (Proverbs 14:23). It is stated a little simpler in the NASB and the NIV: *"Mere talk leads only to poverty."* There is more to real prosperity than just talking a good game. Knowing all the appropriate words and correct lingo is not the answer. There will eventually come a time when you will have to put up or shut up.

I feel like God is saying to many church people today, *"I have heard enough illustrations, now show Me some real-live demonstrations."* So, as we said earlier, *"Don't spill all your beans at any one setting."* That's just an illustration, so save some of your ammo for a real-live demonstration, something that possesses life and strength and purpose and hope.

Talking too much and telling all you know **can cause you to lose your temper**. Look at this: ***"A fool uttereth all his mind"*** (Proverbs 29:11). Now we are back where we started, ***"Don't tell all you know!"*** The latter part of the above cited verse states that *"A wise man keepeth it in till afterwards."*

Let's look at that same verse from the NASB. It is expressed like this: ***"A fool always loses his temper,*** *but a wise man holds it back."* Here is what happens: The prater unloads all he knows and is left abandoned without the proper firearms and ammunition. Then, he has to resort to anger. What else can he do? He blurted it all out in the first three minutes of conversation, etc. What, then, is left in his defense?

It is as though the devil has harassed him to the point of exasperation and then says, "Tell me all you know in five minutes!" It looks as if he has been obedient to the enemy, and has done exactly as commanded. Okay, What has happened? He completely emptied his arsenal in the five minutes he was allotted. What now? What next? He has already played his best hand and the game has only begun. What does he have left? An empty mind and a vile temper. Wow! What a destructive combination! It is loaded with catastrophic influences and, if not conquered, it will lead to his final annihilation.

Another thing that needs to be understood, is that from the beginning to the bitter end, ***the prating fool, is extremely dangerous to himself and others.*** His bite is worse than a rattlesnake! The Bible says of a fool, ***"The beginning of his talking is folly, and the end of it is wicked madness"*** (Ecclesiastes 10:13, NASB). The sacred writer announces the verdict before he declares the outcome of such behavior.

In the previous verse he announces *"The fate of the fool,"* by saying, the lips of a fool will consume him. Then, the next verse continues with what I would call *"The way of the fool:"* *"...The fool multiplies words."* Even though the charges are made, the futility is announced, the verdict is read, and the sentence is passed; the fool continues to multiply words. Then, the solemn question: Where and when will it terminate.

Many times an over zealous and talkative spirit is an evil spirit. The devil enjoys monopolizing the conversation and will do everything he can to keep you 'running off at the mouth.' When you have the floor, when your speech mechanism is in gear, for God's sake, make sure that it is not the devil doing the talking. He will creep into and destroy any conversation when he finds any small crack in the Christian's armor. Satan would just as soon use your voice box, as mine or anyone's, for his soapbox or pulpit. Don't let him do it! There are many times when the Holy Spirit truly desires to scream out loud and say to the speaker, *"SHUT UP!"*

You are going to miss out on a great deal of good things God has for you to use and enjoy, because the motor of your mouth is allowed to run over-time. That 'talkative spirit' can be muzzled and exterminated in the Name of Jesus. You can do it with a little bit of *exertion and exorcism.*

It must also be noted that *the individual who thinks he is religious and does not hold a tight rein on his lip has ample reason to be alarmed* (James 1:26). *His profession is in vain.* If you do not bridle your tongue you are deceived. *You are living a lie!* You "think" you are holy, but you are profane, because you are a part of 'all the above' stated in this discussion about the over-used and the un-controlled tongue. Your inability to supervise your own tongue is also a proof of the worthless-ness (futility and barren-ness, Amp.) of your "religion." It is an exhibition in futility to profess Christianity and let your tongue be loose at both ends.

The Apostle John advised us, *"Love not in word, neither in tongue, but in deed and in truth"* (I John 3:18). This command is nestled in a context of special deeds that exhibit the 'God kind of love' by overt action. Love can lose its power if it is caught up in a whirlwind of hot-air and pointless words. There's got to be a more

4

productive way of expressing the "God kind of love" than by empty words.

If you say you love the Lord, His church, His people and lost people, then do it! That's right, just do it! No excuses. No procrastination. You can always smell the devil's stinking breath when people just talk, and talk, and talk, and…

Jesus saw this type behavior in the people of His day. He left and went to heaven, but they hung around. ***They are still here today.*** He told them, more or less, to avoid this kind of conduct like a plague. Perhaps they did not hear Him, because they still behave the same way. Nevertheless, His word is still in effect. Our Lord's admonition came in *The Sermon On The Mount,* which uses very strong words. It reads like this: ***"When ye pray, use not vain repetitions, as the heathen do: for they think they shall be heard for their much speaking"*** (Matthew 6:7).

It is very interesting to notice how long it takes for some people to learn the truth. After much teaching and experience they have yet to learn that spirituality, knowledge and understanding is not evidenced by long speeches. What Jesus said in the above cited verse comes as a command. It has more bite to it in the NIV, and says, ***"Do not keep on babbling like pagans!"*** And I might add a post script to that: *"It will get you nowhere!"* But Jesus' postscript is much better than mine. ***"The Lord knows what ye have need of before you ask Him."*** Knowledge of what the Lord knows in this case, should trim a great deal of fat off of some of our praying.

Now, let me add a few more verses as an ever present help for controlling the tongue.

First, you must realize the destructive influence of the tongue that is out of control. James says,

"The tongue is a little member and it can boast great things. See how much wood or how great a forest a tiny spark can set ablaze! And the tongue is a fire. (The tongue is a) world of wickedness set among our members, contaminating and depraving the whole body and setting on fire the wheel of birth (the cycle of man's nature), being itself ignited by hell (Gehenna). (James 3:5 & 6, Amp.)

5

Then, follow the direction set by this verse

> *"Let every man be swift to hear; slow to speak, slow to wrath: For the wrath of man worketh not the righteousness of God."*(James 1:19 & 20)

Keep this prayer before God:

> *"Let the words of my mouth and meditation of my heart, be acceptable in Thy sight, O Lord, my rock, and my redeemer."* (Psalm 19:14, NASB)

Chapter 2

You Do Not

Have To Demand Your Rights

Who said you had any rights anyway? You were suppose to have left them at the foot of the cross. Jesus said,

"If any man come after Me, let him deny himself, and take up his cross daily, and follow Me. For whosoever will save his life will lose it; but whosoever will lose his life for my sake, the same shall save it." (Luke 9:23 & 24)

Remember, *"You are not your own, you are bought with a price."* Hopefully, someday, somehow you will mature to the place where you can *distinguish between "rights" and "responsibility."* What do I mean when I say "distinguish between rights and responsibility?

Even though we stated earlier that you should have surrendered your rights at the foot of the cross, be sure to note that you do, indeed, have rights. In his discourse on 'agape,' or, divine love, in I Corinthians 13, Paul shares many characteristics of love. One of these traits, as stated in the Amplified Version, is that, Agape, the real, God kind of love, does not demand it own rights. It is stated like this:

"…Love (God's love in us) does not insist on its own rights, or its own way, for it is not self seeking; it is not touchy or fretful or resentful; it takes no account of evil done to it (it pays no attention to a suffered wrong)". (v.5)

Here is a man who loves God, who knows God, and wrote more of the New Testament than any other writer. He knows the Word! He knows what divine love is all about. He could have demanded many things of the Corinthians, because of 'his rights' and his apostolic order and office. This man also knew that he had the responsibility to love everybody. He responded to their needs rather than insisting on *'his rights'* and privileges.

The Corinthians were constantly challenging Paul's authority and apostleship. Because he truly had this authority, he showed them what he had the 'right' to do because of their attitude and behavior.

The Apostle records what is in his heart in order to teach the fact that although you possess the right to certain privileges you still possess the responsibility to love and minister to those who would attempt to take away those rights. My mind is racing right now to that passage where Paul said, ***"Owe nothing to anyone except to love one another; for he who loves his neighbor has fulfilled the law"*** (Romans 13:8, NASB). Notice how Paul presents his case. It will work for you also.

> ***"Don't I have the right to be given food and drink for my work? Don't I have the right to do what other apostles do, … Are Barnabus and I the only ones that have to work for a living? What soldier ever has to pay his own expenses in the army? What farmer does not eat the grapes from his own vineyard? What shepherd does not use the milk from his own sheep? … We have sown spiritual seed among you. If others have the right to expect this from you, don't we have an even greater right? But we haven't made use of this right. Instead, we have endured everything in order not to put any obstacle in the way of the Good News about Christ….I haven't made use of any of these rights, nor am I writing this now in order to claim such rights for myself. I would rather die first! Nobody is going to turn my rightful boast into empty words."***
> (I Corinthians 9:4 -15, TEV (read on through verse 19, ***POWERFUL***!)

Pregnant women in the United States have the constitutional right to abort their babies, correct? But by the same token they have the moral responsibility to protect that baby and not murder it. Again, people need to learn the difference between rights and responsibilities! They call this particular 'right,' of a woman to abort her unborn child, *'pro-choice.'* Lets pray, for the sake of her soul, and for the child's 'right-to-live,' that she makes the right moral choice. Dear lady, you may be politically correct, but you are spiritually, scripturally, and morally incorrect.

Pro-life activists may have the right to protest the murder of thousands of babies, but they do not have the right to obstruct justice in the way they exercise their 'rights.'

Jesus did not say, *"Demand your rights!"* He said, *"Take up your cross and follow Me daily!"* To take up your cross means to follow Jesus even to the death, if necessary. Let me throw in a word of caution, before you make the choice to take up your cross.

The cross you will have to bear is *not a toothache or an ingrown toe nail*. It is not some physical malady. Taking up 'your' cross is when you reach down, pick up, and shoulder that heavy cross of doing what God has called you to do. Regardless of what it is, take it and walk on! It will be a reproach to many people and they will laugh at you, scorn you, and even attempt to stop you. This can be prevented if you decide to go with the crowd and demand your rights.

The Epistle of James admonishes us by saying, *"Humble yourselves in the sight of the Lord, and He shall lift you up"* (4:10).

God is saying, *"Don't you come in here throwing your weight around, making demands on Me or anyone else! I am the Sovereign God and there is none beside Me. Kneel down over there and shut up!"*

Any individual who demands, commands and reprimands for his "rights" is assaulting and violating the rights of others. Each and every time you demand your rights, you break down the "rights" system by trespassing on another person's rights.

According to Bill Gothard of Basic Life Principles, the best way to handle what you think are your 'rights' is to transfer them to God. You have certain rights because you are the owner of certain items of property. To keep from being selfish about certain 'rights,' turn the ownership of such property over to God. You can trust Him to be a good steward over the welfare of His property.[4] Again, lets look at the difference between rights and responsibility. Here are some scenarios. Check them out.

You have given the ownership of your car to God. Would you say, "Since God owns the car, I do not have to pay the notes on it. I do not have to maintain or keep it in a good state of repair."

Maybe you have given your children over to God. Would you fail to nurture, discipline, educate and see that they have good health care? No! Why? Because you are responsible(?).

You have given your business over to God, right? Would you say, "Since God owns it I do not have to work, I do not have to maintain the business. Since I have given my job to God, I don't have to be concerned about being obedient to my boss, he's in God's hands, I don't have to even show up for work today."

"I have given my wife to God, she doesn't need me to support her now, she's in God's hands."

Don't forget, we do have certain rights and liberties, but we also need to be extremely careful that we do not confuse **liberty** with **license**. Liberty does not give you license (laxity or irresponsibility) to sin. There is the legal side, yes, but there is also a moral one.

Abraham 'had the right' to choose the well watered and fertile plains of the Jordan, but he gave that choice to Lot. Lot exercised 'his rights' and chose the fertile plains and left the desert and wilderness for Abraham.

In his classic and deeply spiritual devotional book, *"My Utmost For His Highest,"* Oswald Chambers, makes a very positive statement concerning the exercise of our personal rights:

"As soon as you begin to live the life of faith in God, fascinating and luxurious prospects will open up before you, and these things are yours by right; but if you are living the life of faith you will exercise your right to waive your rights, and let God choose for you... Whenever right is made the guidance in the life, it will blunt the spiritual insight... Many of us do not go on spiritually because... we prefer to choose what is our right instead of relying on God to choose for us."[5]

The problem with many Christians is that they are so set on demanding and receiving their 'legal or constitutional rights,' they refuse to give up their right to themselves. Your right to yourself is to be surrendered to God. This is what God expects of you if you ever intend to be a disciple of Jesus Christ. If you maintain your right to yourself, your identification is not with Jesus, but with your own ego. Chambers also reminds us that when Jesus calls a disciple, He puts absolute annihilation of the disciple's right to himself, and identification with Jesus, his Lord. This is indeed a relationship with Jesus in which there is no other relationship.[6] I must abdicate the throne of my rights to a reckless abandon of my self and relinquish everything He does not desire. When I demand my rights I choose to accept the good as a substitute for what is best.

One of the biggest problems we have in the United States today is that *we have too many "rights."* The over use and misuse of our rights are eating at the soul of this nation like a cancer. Our founding fathers decreed that we should be endowed with certain unalienable rights, but they did not intend for us to use them to protect ourselves at the expense and exploitation of others. What do you think about a man in prison having 'rights'? He forfeited his rights when he disobeyed the laws of the land and infringed upon someone else's rights. You may be politically correct, but you can also be scripturally, spiritually, and morally wrong.

In his soul-searching autobiography of his life as a missionary, *"Debtor Unashamed,"* Arden Almquist addresses the problem of Americans demanding their rights at the expense of others.[7] He suggests that there is much we can learn from Africans, especially from their communal aspect of living. In his continued discussion on this, he talks about how our 'rugged individualism' has fostered a selfish demand for personal rights. He quotes from a *U. S. News and World Report* article entitled, *"Community And Personal Duty"* (January 28, 1991, p.17). Almquist says that the writer, John Leo, is satirizing American *"rights talk"* and says that Leo is suggesting that our *"obsession with individual rights is making it hard for us to think socially, let alone restore the balance between personal rights and personal obligations...America is more and more coming to look like a random collection of atomized individuals, bristling with rights and choices but with no collected-ness or responsibility for one another."*

When the smoke and dust have settled from the turmoil of the accumulation and acquisition of our 'personal rights,' I wonder if we will feel obligated to help with the cleanup operation. Or will we walk away brushing our hands and saying, *"They do not have the right to leave all this debris in my path! I don't have to put up with this! My constitutional rights guarantee me a smooth road to walk throughout all my life!"*

Gothard was correct in telling us we need to surrender our rights. And through that, offers a good solution to those individuals who are plagued with the problem of demanding their rights. He suggested that yielding our rights is an act of meekness.[8] Jesus said, *"Blessed are the meek: for they shall inherit the earth"* (Matthew 5:5). Jesus Himself is the source of that meekness and He invites us to seek Him for it (Matthew 11:28 & 29).

The people that think the world owes them a living, and are demanding their rights, would take the whole world if they thought they could get it through probate court.

Who are the meek? They are those who yield all possessions and personal rights to God and thereafter look upon what they have as loaned to them by God for His work and glory.

Those who *'must have their rights'* get angry if they feel *'their rights'* have been violated. Anger, according to Gothard, is the opposite of meekness. There is no place in the re-created and blood-bought human heart for both anger and meekness. *"Either we have one as our basic nature, or we have the other."* - Gothard

Anger is the immediate reaction to a personal rights violation. And to quote Gothard again, "It would not be possible to have a conflict with someone unless personal rights were involved."[9]

This is a wonderful place to inject another fact, *Meekness is not weakness*. It is not humility, although a meek person is humble. In the spirit realm meekness exhibits a strength not shown in humility. You might run over an humble person, but not so with a meek individual. Study the life of Moses, the Bible says,

"...The man Moses was very meek, above all the men which were upon the face of the earth" (Numbers 12:3)

The following warning goes from one missionary to another, but I feel it is good counsel for anyone who truly desires to be a servant of God.

"On the mission field it is not the enduring of hardships, the lack of comforts, and the roughness of the life that make the missionary cringe and falter. It is something far less romantic and far more real. It is something that will hit you right down where you live. The missionary has to give up having his own way. He has to give up

having any rights. He has, in the words of Jesus, to 'deny himself.' [10] He must give up himself, that's exactly what Jesus did. He had the 'right' to call 10 leagues of angels to deliver Him from the horrors of the crucifixion, ***BUT NO!* This was His moment! It was the reason for which He came!** The whole world had been waiting for this moment. He came to die on the cross. *If Jesus had exercised His 'rights' it would have jeopardized your salvation and mine for all time and eternity.*

Chapter 3

You Do Not

Have To Avenge Yourself

Vengeance belongs to God. You couldn't really get even with anyone if you wanted to. Don't retaliate, that is God's business. You do not need to argue or engage yourself in any kind of defensive dialogue. *"Vengeance belongeth unto Me, I will recompense, saith the Lord"* (Hebrews 10:30). Attempting to avenge yourself is an expensive and futile experience that can render nothing that would be of any permanent and positive spiritual value. Attend to your own business, not God's!

As a born-again child of God, you are admonished to be patient, so believe what God has said. When you attempt to avenge yourself you are, as it were, saying, "God is a liar, He will not vindicate me." The proper thing to do, when the temptation comes to get even, is to let the demons roar. The temptation is only lying, clamoring voices, inside your mind, that accuse you. They tell you that you have to strike back. But remember, *Satan is the accuser of the brethren, God is the Avenger.*

It is my understanding that, as Christians, we are to turn the other cheek or go the second mile when assaulted by the enemy in this manner. By behaving in this fashion you provide God with all the space He needs to come to your rescue with His vengeance.

Has it ever occurred to you that your desire to avenge yourself is *Vigilante Christianity? "A vigilante is a member of a group that sets itself up without authority to seek out and punish crime"* (Webster). Did you know there are vigilantes in the Body of Christ? They are easy to detect, because they are constantly trying to get even. Yes, get even with the pastor, other members of the church and people that believe doctrines different from their own. These vigilantes are continually on a crusade to get revenge on someone. It looks as though they cannot find the victory with which to forgive and forget. Because of their hidden guilt or hurt they set themselves up to police the church. Really, it is a form of rebellion because they do not have the authority to do so. They are like the Ku Klux Klan, taking the law into their own hands.

Many times these spirits come into an individual when he or she has been hurt or wronged, and, in most cases, they are not even aware that demon forces are working through them.

To prevent this kind of conduct be sure you do not harbor unforgiveness, resentment, bitterness or grudges in your heart. Release them immediately! When you release any one of them, and begin to forgive you will recognize what Gothard says, that "bitterness is assuming a right you do not have."[11] To be healed, pray against these spirits and rebuke them in the Name of Jesus and be sure to forgive everyone you think might have wronged you in any way.

The Apostle Paul can teach this lesson much better than I, so learn from him on this matter.

"Don't pay back a bad turn by a bad turn, to anyone. See that your public behavior is above criticism. As far as your responsibility goes, live at peace with everyone. Never take vengeance into your own hands, my dear friends: stand back and let God punish as He desires. For it is written:

Vengeance belongeth unto Me: I will recompense, saith the Lord.

As it is also written:

If thine enemy hunger, feed him;

If he thirst, give him drink:

For in so doing thou shalt heap coals of fire upon his head. Don't allow yourself to be overpowered by evil. Take the offensive and overpower evil with good."

(Romans 12:17-21, Phillips)

Chapter 4

You Do Not

Have To Be Important

So be real. Act yourself. Remember, you are what you are and nothing more. Isn't it surprising how extremely 'important' some people become when they receive even a small amount of authority or responsibility. If you could buy this individual for what he is actually worth and sell him for what he thinks he is worth, you would receive an enormous return on your investment. You do not have to be eminent, prominent, or notable. Quit trying to look important! Be sure to avoid that type of temptation at all costs. Being important is a very expensive luxury you cannot afford.

If you attempt to be important you will not grow spiritually. You will not bring glory to God. You will not advance His cause and kingdom in any positive, constructive, permanent or productive way. Remember, Jesus said that those who were not with Him were against Him. If you are trying to be important, you are not building HIS Kingdom, you are on a collision course to frustration, striving to build you own empire.

What about these people who are so important that they do not have time for people? Are you so important that you don't want people to see you out side your office? Are you so important you don't want people to know your telephone number? If you are going to be worth anything in the advancement of the Kingdom of God, you are going to have to be a 'people' person.

In our missionary agency office we, like many others, stay extremely busy. Some people visit our office just to sit and talk. This is especially true when it seems that we are the busiest. What do you do in a situation like that? Okay, do we go into our private offices and leave these people unattended? Do we say we have too much work to do to visit with them? Do we say, in a proud and 'super-spiritual' way, "This is God's business and we must get on with 'the work at hand'!? Do you let them go on hurting while you enjoy the pleasure of 'being about the Father's business'? We decided early on that we are in the "people business," and we are going to afford them the dignity of being who they are, and can be in Christ.

We are never too busy to spend time with people. God is in the people business. Jesus died for PEOPLE and I hope we will never become so important that we do not have time for them.

People try to be important because they do not think they are important. They need to realize that Jesus considered them important enough to lay down His life for them.

The Bible speaks directly to 'important people'. Listen to Solomon again, *"Do not claim honor in the presence of the king, and do not stand in the place of great men."* (Proverbs 25:6 & 7, NASB). Jesus has a solution for the kind of problem we are dealing with. It is very simple: don't exalt yourself, don't try to be important and don't look or sound important. If you do, you will receive your guaranteed demotion. Jesus can enforce it. *"Everyone who makes himself great will be humbled..."* (Luke 14:11, TEV)

Many professionals are too busy. But regardless of their 'busy-ness,' and the overcrowded schedules, they still need to take time for people. Don't make them wait because you think you are too busy, or because you are more important than they are. Those people who are waiting on you are busy also. They have crowded schedules too. They are important also. You gave them an appointment. They came because you said "I can see you *at this time.*" I know some appointments take longer than others, but I am also aware that some of you take more than one appointment for only one appointment time. The *reason* you do that is not to be discussed here, but yet it happens. Those other 'professionals,' who are waiting on you, are busy also. They set their schedule because you gave your word, on the time of the appointment. But, since you are so important, they had to operate according to your schedule, not theirs.

If you are in the ministry of Jesus Christ, whether Apostle, Prophet, Evangelist, Pastor, Teacher, Missionary, etc., *God forbid that you should think of yourself as a celebrity.* You are a servant. If you are too important to serve tables you are too important to serve God. And, whatever you are, you are that, by the grace of God (I Corinthians 15:10). If it is beneath your dignity to clean toilets, you are too important for God.

Be sure to double check your mind and motive. Be sure to control the thoughts and intents of your heart (Heb. 4:12), so you can be sure of this also: Set a guard over your lips and be careful about the overuse of personal pronouns, such as *'I, me, my.'* Extravagant flaunting of these pronouns betrays and exposes your carnal desire to 'be important.'

Mrs. Charles E. Cowan, in her classic devotional book, *"Springs In The Valley,"* gives us a quote from a Moravian prayer that I would recommend to anyone who is experiencing ego problems. The prayer reads like this, *"From the desire of being great, good Lord deliver us."*[12] This prayer needs to be prayed continually until the symptoms have disappeared and the urge to be great and important no longer haunt you.

Chapter 5

You Do Not

Have To Play The Grandstands

Take off that mask, you hypocrite! Let people get exactly what they see. Who do you think you are fooling? Remember what President Abraham Lincoln said? "You may fool some of the people all the time, and all the people some of the time, but you cannot fool all the people all the time." And I might add… you cannot fool God at any time. Some of the people that you might think you can con or fool may have God's Spirit dwelling in them. They are going to read your mail and know beyond the shadow of a doubt, that you are a fraud, a hoax, and a phony.

Christians truly need to be careful hustling this part of the devil's garbage. You could easily become one of his con artists. It is fleshly and carnal to desire to impress others, and doing such could cause an evil spirit of manipulation to come upon you and overpower you.

Don't think that if you are a con artist, you are someone to be praised because you possess some degree of intelligence or special wisdom that others do not possess. Really it is the height of ignorance, you are a puppet of the devil and you need to be set free from this satanic strangle hold. There is authority in the Name of Jesus that can bring about the deliverance you so desperately need.

Hey, get honest! Come clean! Its high time you became transparent! You have been vague and vain long enough. There is one thing for sure, down under all that fabrication and facade is a real person that the Lord has made and truly loves. That particular individual bears your name. If you truly become honest with yourself and God, you would readily recognize the fact that you have no desire to live all your life in a fraudulent, false, and phony mode.

This kind of lifestyle makes you a bond-servant to those you are attempting to influence and persuade. Satan calls the signals, and you, as his vassal, run the plays. The Bible says you belong to the power you choose to obey (Romans 6:16).

It is rather comical to watch someone try to impress others. Did you ever see a teenage boy when he is trying to smoke for the first time in public? And if you *really* want to see a comedy, watch a woman smoke in public.

Hey, it doesn't matter, because what they see is what they get. There's a bottom line down there somewhere and somebody will eventually get to it. If you just let these performers alone they will soon fall by their own weight somewhere, somehow, sometime, and great will be their fall. This is simply because they erected their building on a miserable, pitiful, and wretched foundation. Jesus aimed straight to the heart of those individuals who are vaccinated with this booster shot of satanic toxin. Look closely at what He had to say about these people whose only hope for survival is to play the grandstands with their heads in the clouds.

"Beware of doing your good deeds conspicuously to catch men's eyes or you will miss the reward of your Heavenly Father. So, when you do good to other people, don't hire a trumpeter to go in front of you-like those play actors in the synagogues and streets who make sure that men admire them. Believe Me they have all the reward they are going to get." (Matthew 6:1, Phillips)

Any individual who attempts to play the grandstands really does not know what real importance actually is. He is fooling himself in the process. He is wasting his time, energy, and very possibly, his salvation, peddling this piece of the devil's garbage. If you are a minister of the Gospel of Jesus Christ, don't you believe your time could be better spent doing Godly things rather than trying to satisfy the desires of the flesh?

Preachers and ministers who give evangelistic or inflated reports, glowing with the thousands saved, healed and delivered and with the "beyond biblical" results, distort the facts and mislead God's flock. People who resort to this form of *"Hyperbolic Christianity"* are interested only in drawing attention to their own self importance and making an all-out effort to justify their existence. It is nothing more than spiritual manipulation.

Unfortunately, this ungodly exaggeration will filter down into the flock, infecting the converts with a spirit of deception and leading them down the wrong road to the place where some of them may never return.

Chapter 6
You Do Not
Have To Prove Yourself

No, you do not have to prove that you are right, even if you are. Don't you know that truth will eventually prevail? Is it worth all the fighting and trouble that you might go through just to prove your intelligence or to prove that your opinion was better? Who are you trying to fool, God or man? There are those that would fight till they die just to prove themselves right or to prove someone else wrong. Do you really think it's worth it? What have you accomplished if you go to the trouble and expense to prove yourself right? Have you influenced the cause of Christ by proving your brother to be wrong? Is it really to your advantage or his to embarrass him? The Bible says, *"Study to show thyself approved UNTO GOD, a workman that needeth not to be ashamed, rightly dividing the word of truth"* (II Timothy 2:15).

So I would simply advise you by saying, *"Be not deceived, God is not mocked, for whatsoever a man soweth, that shall he also reap"* (Galatians 6:7).

Hey, you are just like the rest of us, you ain't perfect! You are only human. So what if you do foul up? What if you do make a mistake? Get in line with the rest of us. You will cause a great deal of heartache if you continue to try to prove yourself. So, please ponder this: someone else will suffer while you are enjoying the pleasure of proving your point. By the way, don't you think your record (testimony) will speak for itself? Anyway, its better to look stupid than to open your mouth and confirm it.

The $64,000 dollar question is this: Why are you so determined to prove yourself to be right? It probably would not hurt a thing if you should happen to be wrong sometime. What is driving you? Where is the pressure coming from that makes you think you just have to 'be right?'

I am again indebted to Chambers at this juncture, because he has given a very important diagnosis of this *"I'M-important"* disease. He says that an insistence in proving we are right is nearly always an indication that there has been some point of disobedience."[13] I would suggest that you just let it alone. It will surface somewhere.

Chapter 7

You Do Not

Have To Tell A More Exciting Story

Is it absolutely necessary for you to tell a bigger fish story? Wake up and realize nobody is crowding you and you are under no legitimate pressure to compete with anyone. This is not a contest. Who said you had to top the previous story? So, don't blow their ship completely out of the water with your tall tales. If you are an older Christian, and have had more experiences, don't compete with the younger person in Christ. You could easily monopolize the entire conversation and others would be reluctant to share. Why? Your extravagant stories have made them feel inferior and they think they have no contribution to make in this exaggerated exhibition of yarns. Instead of preventing others from participating in gainful discussions, do all you can to engage their input. This will encourage their growth, but to blow them away with exotic and eccentric bragging will stunt their growth. Their advance to Christian maturity will be hindered, now or later, especially when they learn that what you have led them to think, by your talkative spirit, was incorrect. Your experience can truly be a witness and an encouragement to others if you get your motives and attitudes right.

Fabricated stories have no place in your preaching, teaching, or casual discourse. Be sure to resist the temptation to add colorful scenarios, and descriptive adjectives that will enhance the grandeur of your splendid speech. It ain't worth it. For God's sake don't do like Jesus said of the heathens: *Who use vain repetitions, ...who "think they shall be heard for their much speaking"* (Matthew 6:7). If this type behavior is yours, *I cannot say, "I'm impressed!* Many Christians are wondering if you will ever outgrow this juvenile lifestyle.

Our tall tales can actually create illusions of grandeur that cause young believers to get a false picture of the gospel. It is a work of the flesh (lying) motivated by pride and the desire to control others by your self-proclaimed importance.

It would be much cheaper for you to stay at home instead of being away all the time on these expensive ego trips. I feel sure that you have no desire for your life to be bloated, and, neither do you have a desire to build your reputation on exaggeration. So, in order to prevent yourself from working to receive this kind of consequence, *be sure to 'tell it like it is'.* You don't have to play that silly game of "Can you top this?" That is one game we do not need to know how to play.

When we witness for Jesus we are personal representatives of Him, not substitutes for Him. When you represent Someone there is no need for self-justification. And the bottom line is "self," when you argue or become more extravagant with the stories you tell.

Chapter 8

You Do Not

Have To Get Offended

The word 'offense' in its various forms comes forth in the New Testament from many directions. Offenses have the appearance of electricity. They have 'plus' and 'minus' charges. Offenses have a very shocking effect on anyone who deals with them. They can have 'positive' and 'negative' results. To be extremely honest, offenses are charged with volatile contrasts. That's the reason I said earlier that they come from many directions. The same phenomenon/occurrence will have different responses from different people. Let's look at some of these contrasts.

Offenses Can Produce Either 'Woes' or 'Blessings'

WOES.

Jesus said, "Woe to the world because of its stumbling blocks! For it is inevitable that stumbling blocks come; but woe to that man through whom the stumbling block comes"! (Matthew 18:7, NASB)

The phrase *"stumbling blocks"* in the NASB (Luke 17:1) is called *"temptations to sin"* or *"influences to do wrong,"* in the Amplified Version. In the NIV it is called *"things that cause people to sin."* Another way of stating the meaning of "stumbling blocks" is that they are **"SOLICITATIONS TO SIN."** Jesus is simply saying, "Make no mistake about it, temptations, stumbling blocks, opportunities to get offended will indeed come." Jesus is alerting every individual to be ready and prepared so as not to yield to the temptations and become the victims of the 'woes' that will leave them bleeding by the side the road.

Christians know that Satan is going to throw these stumbling blocks in the path before them as they move forward in Christ. Let's prevent as many 'woes' as possible, for ourselves and those we love.

BLESSINGS.

Offenses can also bring blessings. The Prophet, John the Baptist, was in prison. He sent some of his disciples to Jesus with this inquiry:

"Are you the long awaited Messiah or shall we keep looking for another?" Jesus sent word back to the Prophet and gave him a report of the things that were happening wherever He ministered. The miracles should have shown them that this Man was indeed the Messiah. But Jesus added an extra line or two to His report to John.

> *"...Blessed (happy fortunate, and to be envied) is he who takes no offense at Me and finds no cause for stumbling in and through Me and is not hindered from seeing the Truth."*
> (Matthew 11:6, Amp.)

Some (many) people actually stumble at Jesus because, in most cases, He is a threat to their attitude and lifestyle. This is the reason the Name of Jesus provokes such hostilities. This verse happens to be another of our Lord's Beatitudes. It is as though Jesus is saying, "How happy are those who will not allow Me nor the things I stand for to cause them to get bent all out of shape and sin against Me or anyone else" (author's paraphrase).

Offenses Can Come From Either God Or Satan

God offended Cain (Genesis 4:1 - 12) and he became angry with God, because God did not respect Cain's selfish offering. He offended David (II Samuel Chapter 6). David was upset with God because His wrath was broken out against Uzzah. Jesus offended His own family (John 7:5 - 8). They did not believe Him. Their offense came because they didn't like the bad press Jesus was giving to the family because of His unorthodox mannerisms, doctrines, and some of the company He kept. Jesus offended the Pharisees very frequently. On one occasion His disciples came to Him and asked if He knew He had offended the Pharisees. It did not bother the Lord that He had offended them. He had purposely provoked them (Matthew 15:12). In fact, Jesus' reply to His disciples was, *"...Every plant, which My heavenly Father hath not planted shall be rooted up. Let them alone: They be blind leaders of the blind. And if the blind lead the blind, both shall fall into the ditch"* (Matthew 15:13 & 14). He offended Mary and Martha (John chapter 11). Mary and Martha were both offended at Jesus because He was not present before Lazarus died. They both reprimanded Him for not coming. Because, they thought 'He could have healed Lazarus and prevented his death.' Check these stories out and notice how each person in each case reacted to Jesus. Please notice and remember that God can do whatever He desires. Many of these people were offended because God did not do what they had desired. He did not do it the way they wanted it. But, you know, **God does not have to do anything the same way twice.** He can do whatever He desires, whether we like it or not.

Try to see your offender as a special envoy from God to do a work in your life. The brothers of Joseph who sold him into slavery were jealous and did what they could to bring harm to him. But in the end, when Joseph became prime minister of Egypt, and his brothers realized the authority he possessed, they repented. They fell on their faces before their brother and begged forgiveness. Joseph's brothers were his offenders, but he refused to be offended. He told his fainthearted brothers, *"Ye thought to do evil against me; but God meant it unto good, ...to save much people alive"* (Genesis 50:20). Joseph's own brothers were God's special agents to use Joseph to do a great work. These evil offenders were used of God.

You may also desire to read in II Samuel 16:5 - 11 where an offender was sent to curse King David. He was of the tribe of Benjamin of the family of Saul and was bitter against David. When the servants of the king desired to kill this man, David said, *"...Let him alone, and let him curse, for the Lord hath bidden him"* (v. 11). David refused to be offended because his offender was sent from God.

Whenever the Pharisees offended people it was most always from Satan. They were the devil's advocates and special agents of offense.

Offenses Can Either Be 'Active' or 'Passive'

You can be the **Offender** or you can be the *Offended*. If you are the offender, make sure your motives are right and that your heart is pure before God. Remember what Jesus said about the offender. He said 'woe,' to the one through whom or by whom the offenses come. Jesus was careful to instruct His followers to beware of offending others. **He issues a very solemn warning about offending babes in Christ.**

He said, *"...Whosoever shall offend one of these little ones that believe in Me, it is better for him that a millstone were hanged about his neck, and he were cast into the sea."* (Mark 9:42)

You never know how much damage can be done to those you offend. Solomon speaks to the issue also and says, *"A brother offended is harder to be won than a strong city"* (Proverbs 18:19, NASB).

Are you aware of what happened to Cain after he was offended at God (Genesis 4:1-12)? *First* of all, his vile temper drove him to murder his own brother. *Next,* he came under a curse from the very ground that opened up to receive the blood of his brother. Cain very possibly opened himself up to demon possession. *Then,* he became a fugitive and a vagabond to roam aimlessly to and fro upon the earth, "in perpetual exile, a degraded outcast" (Amp.).

I wonder how many people have been offended by 'good church folks' and left the church, possibly, never to return. They could easily have a vile temper like Cain, speak death or offend others, become demon possessed, and become a spiritual tramp never finding a place to roost, rest, repent, and be reconciled.

Such things as these are no doubt what prompted the Apostle Paul to admonish the church at Rome about offenders. His warning note was this:

"I urge you, brothers, to watch out for those who cause division and put obstacles in your way that are contrary to the teaching you have learned. Keep away from them. For such people are not serving our Lord Christ, but their own appetites. By smooth talk and flattery they deceive the minds of naive people." (Romans 16:17 & 18, NIV)

And, if your heart is not pure, you can easily *be* offended. When the Jews built their house, they left out the 'Chief Cornerstone,' which was Jesus Christ. Jesus was to them a *"Stone of stumbling and a Rock of offense."* They stumbled over that stumbling block, and were offended at Jesus, because He did not meet their specifications of the Messiah. The Apostle Peter said of the Jews, They ...*"stumbled at the Word, being disobedient..."* (I Peter 2:8). The Jews were appointed to a special place in God's Kingdom, but they got offended and missed it.

The word in the Greek from which the word 'offense' is derived is '*skandalon*.' This was a part of a trap or a snare. Really, *"It was the part of the trap where the bait is attached."* 'Skandalon' is always *used metaphorically, and ordinarily of anything that arouses prejudice, or becomes a hindrance to others, or causes them to fall by the way."*[14] It should also be noted that sometimes the offense is in itself good, and those stumbled by it are wicked. That part of the trap where the bait is attached is the enticing part that lures the victim into it jaws.

In the Amplified Version, Matthew states the inevitability of the coming offenses like this, *"It is necessary that temptations come."* Then, in the same version, it reads thusly: *"... Temptations (snares, traps set to entice to sin) are sure to come"* (Luke 17:1). Be sure to prepare yourself because offenses are indeed coming your way. Offenses started with Cain and they continue today and you are not exempt from their aggressive assaults. You will, no doubt, have to deal with them everyday. I must confess, this has been a fox I have had to deal with as much as any. I trust someday to have a heart void of offense.

The bait set before the prospective victim is very appealing and very seductive in its charm. Beware! *You can take the bait or let it alone.* You do not have to take it! But, if you do, you will be offended. So, from here on we will deal with the offended and not the offender, because it is our purpose to tell you that you do not have to be offended. This is one of the little foxes that will set your fields on fire.

Jesus said offenses will come. You know that, by now, I trust. So, let me just give you this admonition for your own benefit. *If you are offendable, you will be offended!* Also, take note of this, *the less offendable you are the more you can be used of God.* That is the reason for His putting offenses in your path. He wants you and others to see you get offended and to allow you to be ashamed for your behavior. He wants others to see you offended so that they, as well as yourself, can see its vile and vicious nature. God also wants you to grow up and rise above this juvenile behavior.

We get offended when someone challenges our security, safety, comfort, knowledge, position, judgment, authority, etc. Keep your antennas up and when anyone challenges you on these or any other matters, *don't take the bait!*

If you are one of those who exhibits your feelings on your shoulders, for God's sake get some help! Get healed! Get delivered!

You need to know that God will punish the offender. He said, *"Vengeance is Mine, I will repay, saith God."* It is indeed noteworthy, at this point, to share this command from God: *"Do not let the sun go dawn while you are still angry"* (Ephesians 4:26, NIV). I trust you can see the serious peril of walking on this treacherous ground of being so sensitive and getting offended so easily.

Jesus gave a parable about offenses in Matthew 13:20 & 21. It is one segment of the Parable of the Sower. It deals with the seed that was sown in stony places. Jesus compared this portion of the parable to those individuals who hear the Word and by and by receive it into their hearts. Like the ground that was full of rocks, their hearts are hard and stony. Because of all the rocks in their hearts they have no depth of soil for the seed to really take root. Oh, it germinates and springs up alright, but the young, tender plant stands and looks good for awhile, but has insufficient ground for the seed (Word) to take root and get established. Later, when affliction, trouble, or persecution comes because of the Word, they get offended.

How well established are you in the Word? There is no doubt about it, you definitely need to be established in the Word. It will renew your mind and put you on a solid foundation. This behooves me to ask you this question: "What are you going to do when you are: rejected, misquoted, misunderstood, lied about and belittled by whatever forces that would attempt to offend you? Are you going to take the bait or let it alone?"

On one of our missionary team trips to a certain third-world country we were enjoying each other's fellowship in the Lord. After our fellowship time was over, someone said to the group, *"These people are easily offended, you need to apologize to them."* Someone else said, *"Why, what's wrong?"* The answer was, *"They are easily offended, and it's part of their culture."* And then another team member spoke up said, *"They may think it is cultural, but it is demonic!"* To say it is cultural, conditional, or customary is a cop-out or an escape-hatch to avoid the issue.

When you are easily offended you are hiding something in your heart. Whatever you are covering up, uncover it and get rid of it! Grow up! How long are you going to cover up your sin by blaming someone else for all your sin, hang-ups, and demonic possession? No one will ever satisfy you as long as you keep harboring your problems. People get tired of having to walk lightly around you because they think they will hurt your feelings.

Please allow the Word of God to be your help in this matter. Christians who have their minds renewed by the Word, are bolstered with extra strength and ammunition to help them stand when offenses come.

God has a very valuable gift He desires to pass on to you, it is called *'love.'* It is called *'charity'* in the KJV, or *'agape.'* Jesus confused the minds of the New Testament world by springing on them the God kind of love. They could not understand this thing called 'agape." The people of Jesus' day were used to 'an eye for an eye,' mentality. They knew nothing about a love that would keep on loving without expecting a reward in return. Jesus taught them about a love that did not provoke retaliation. Paul, in writing about 'agape,' said, *"It is not rude nor selfish," nor "quick to take offense,"... and "keeps no score of wrongs"* (I Corinthians 13:5, NEB).

When Paul was being tried by Felix the Governor, he stood in his own defense. And while speaking on behalf of his innocence, he gave a glowing testimony for God. That special testimony brought out a special characteristic from his own heart, which would be good for all of us to duplicate.

"...I always exercise and discipline myself [mortifying my body, deadening my carnal affections, bodily appetites, and worldly desires, endeavoring in all respects] to have a clear (unshaken, blameless) conscience, void of offense toward God and toward men." (Acts 24:16, Amp.)

In closing, let's look at what the Psalmist said about this matter: *"Great peace have they that love thy law, and nothing shall offend them"* (Psalm 119:165). Evidently, the Word of God is one of the best insurance policies to help protect us when we are presented with opportunities to get offended.

Chapter 9

You Do Not

Have To Win The Argument

It doesn't matter how right you are, you still do not have to win the argument. When you confront or summons an individual and come against his opinions or sentiments, you will challenge him to a duel. You put him on the defense and his guard goes up. You have provoked him and he is ready to fight. The more you challenge, the more he becomes defensive. Every time you prevail upon him, the greater will be his determination to retaliate. He will retreat, temporarily, return to his arsenal, and prepare for a greater offensive. And on it goes, back and forth, with a continuous offense, from one side to the other. You are in it, and you may even win it, but never forget this: *"YOU CAN WIN THE BATTLE AND LOSE THE WAR."* The best thing to do is not to allow yourself to get manipulated into this kind of useless dialogue.

Many times in 'one-on-one evangelism,' the evangelist lets his client seduce him into an exchange of fruitless debate over dogma, denominations, and doctrines. And because the evangelist is grounded and founded in scripture and is well versed in 'churchianity,' he wins the argument. Unfortunately, he loses his client in the very pleasure of winning the debate. And sadly, the client goes on his way to eternity without Jesus Christ. This kind of triumph is one luxury we cannot afford. The stakes are too high. Don't, for God's sake, *don't allow the devil to pull you over to the sidelines into a sparring match that will cause you to defend yourself at the expense of a precious soul Jesus died to redeem!* It isn't worth it. For that individual, Jesus shed His blood in vain. Why? Because you could not resist the temptation to be a victor. Yes, you became the *victor* and your client became the *victim.* Remember, *there is only one, real, true victor!* Don't try to take the victory from Him, just relax in His victory. That's the way we win in God's economy.

The situations we are dealing with in this study admonish us to know that we should never feel compelled to be competitive. This is not a contest. It is the real way of life. Thus far in this study, and maybe even later, an unwritten implication floats along as we read. It's a challenge. You should never allow yourself to be manipulated into competition, regardless of its category. If you keep in close touch with your spirit, and therefore, with the Holy Spirit, you know that you do not have to get into a conflict with anyone. Don't allow Satan to seduce you into any kind of a rivalry with himself or any of his cohorts.

The enemy will even use the individual you are witnessing to, to entice you into an argument. Be wise as a serpent and harmless as a dove and head the devil off at the pass.

Some people are intimidated by another person's performance and/or behavior and might be seduced into competition with that other person's worship, prayer, singing, etc. *For God's sake, wake up and wise up and don 't be snared into one of the devil's traps.* It is so unnecessary, because *"We are not ignorant of Satan's devices"* (2 Corinthians 2:11). Why don't we just beat him at his own game? Don't argue, just allow him to blow his stack and get scalded by his own steam. Give him enough rope and he will hang himself.

Chapter 10

You Do Not

Have To Keep Up With The Jones'

When will you ever learn, God doesn't want you keeping up with the Jones. He has been trying to steer you in a different direction. He is also working with the Jones and trying to get them to move in the direction He desires for them to go. Besides, God has explicitly told Christians not to covet. If you have to have a car as big or bigger than them, you truly need to check your motives and attitudes. Something could be wrong that causes you to desire to compete.

Who or what causes you to want to keep up with the Jones? Who do you think it will impress? Pastor, does your steeple need to be taller than the church down the street or across town? Will it bring greater eternal results? Does it make you look less prosperous or successful than your friends if your house is not as big as theirs or is not in that more affluent section of town? Will your new Cadillac, Lincoln Town Car, or Mercedes transport you to your destination any quicker, any safer, or more comfortably than my little '89 Cutlass Cierra? Jesus said, *"Take heed, and beware of covetousness: FOR A MAN'S LIFE CONSISTETH NOT IN THE ABUNDANCE OF THINGS WHICH HE POSSESSETH"* (Luke 12:15). Wake up! Your eternal destiny is not weighed in the balances of the things you possess.

"Be ye, therefore, followers of God as dear children: and walk in love, as Christ also hath loved us, and hath given Himself for us an offering and a sacrifice to God for a sweet smelling savor. But fornication, and all uncleanness, or COVETOUSNESS, LET IT NOT BE ONCE NAMED AMONG YOU, AS BECOMETH SAINTS; neither filthiness, nor foolish talking, nor jesting, which are not convenient (fitting): but, rather, giving of thanks." (Ephesians 5:2)

The previous words were written by the Apostle Paul to the church at Ephesus, and he said, among other things, of covetousness, "LET IT NOT BE ONCE NAMED AMONG YOU." Covetousness is not to be allowed to filter into our thoughts, words, and deeds, *NO, NOT EVEN ONCE!*

Also to the Colossians, he was even more adamant about such ungodliness, he said, *"Put it to death, ... whatever belongs to your earthly nature: sexual immorality, impurity, lust, evil desires, GREED, which is idolatry"* (3:5). He is saying that covetousness or greed, which is listed among many other abominable sins, **"PUT IT TO DEATH, IT IS IDOLATRY!"** What if the Jones are going to the poor house? or to jail? or to the morgue? or to hell? If you are hustling this load of the devil's junk, unload it NOW! This little fox will set your fields of life and ministry on fire!

Make a serious search of your heart about attitudes and activities concerning your motives in these matters. Make another serious search of the scriptures and determine the legitimacy of the greed, covetousness, desire for things, and the competitive spirit of this kind of conduct. If you can get God's approval for this kind of spirit and demeanor, go ahead with it. But you must remember, *God and His Word are one, and never the twain shall separate.*

Rid yourself of this competitive spirit immediately, in the Name of Jesus! Where did you get the idea that you had to compete with anyone. When you compete you are working an injustice on yourself, on your self-inflicted (that's right, *you created him*) competitor, and on others concerned. All of this type of competition is grossly unnecessary and totally absurd.

Chapter 11

You Do Not

Have To Worry

It is a sin to worry anyway. Jesus was very explicit in cautioning individuals about worrying or being anxious about their livelihood, etc. This advice and warning is found in our Lord's "Sermon on The Mount" (Matthew 6:25, 28, 31 & 34). Some scholars have said that this "Sermon" (Matthew chapters 5, 6, & 7) is *"The Law of the New Testament."* Jesus is very rigid in His presentation and very demanding in His expectations. In spite of His stern presentation, our Lord offered a very valuable alternative to this thing called "worry." It is found within the context of His rebuke to those who would betray their lack of faith through their alarm and anxious concern. Jesus made it very simple in explaining the fact that God already knows their need, whatever it might be. He spoke boldly and said, **"worrying is what the heathen do." Christians do not have to resort to this kind of anti-trust.** His prescription for worrying was this:

"...Seek (aim at and strive after) first of all His Kingdom and His righteousness (His way of doing and being right), and then all these things taken together will be given you besides. So do not worry or be anxious about tomorrow, for tomorrow will have worries and anxieties of its own. Sufficient for each day is its own trouble." (Matthew 6:33 & 34, Amp.)

You are actually burning expensive midnight oil that you could save if you would quit worrying. When you worry you are disobeying Jesus and, again you are peddling the devil's merchandise which will cause your hair to turn gray and give you an ulcerated stomach. It is much simpler to obey Jesus and make your primary goal that of seeking the Kingdom of God. The things you could have been worrying about, would be given to you collectively, if you would simply obey God and His Word. Read Matthew 6:33 & 34 again and meditate on it.

The Apostle Paul also saw the futility of worrying. He, like Jesus said, **"DON'T DO IT!"** Here is the way he put it:

"Do not fret or have any anxiety about anything, but in every circumstance and in everything, by prayer and petition (definite requests), with thanksgiving, continue to make your wants known to God." (Philippians 4:6, Amp.)

"In every circumstance and in everything." That covers it all. That leaves you exactly nothing to worry about. Some people go on the assumption of "Why pray when you can worry?" But the adverse of that is what Paul is attempting to get us to grasp. So, remember, to worry is to sin against God. It's much less expensive and more profitable just to pray.

"Each day," Jesus said, *"will have enough of its own problems without you adding yesterday's and tomorrow's to it."* He did not say, "worry without ceasing," His word does command us to "pray without ceasing." This is one of several ways to prevent worrying. It would most definitely be profitable for you, spiritually, mentally and physically, *"to pray and obey."* This is how Pastor Cho built the largest church in the world in Seoul, Korea, *"praying and obeying."*

Chapter 12

You Do Not

Have To Be Concerned About Who Gets The Credit

Don't get bent out of shape about who gets the credit. In the final analysis it is God who gets all the credit and glory, anyway. So, just sit tight and allow God to work it out His way. The devil cannot do a thing to you unless God allows it. Pilate, the Roman governor, was already trembling with fear, when Jesus stood before him to be tried. And, because the Lord did not answer him the way Pilate desired, he became adamantly upset at the Lord. And in his fury, Pilate shouted out at Jesus and said, *"Don't you know that I have the power to put You to death or to set you free!"* Jesus answered, **"Thou couldest have no power at all against Me, except it were given thee from above"** (John 19:11).

What the Lord was conveying to Pilate was the fact that it really didn't matter what Pilate thought or did, God was still in control. Jesus could care less about what Pilate had the power to do. Pilate could do nothing unless God allowed or permitted it. Regardless of what you or I do, whether we get the credit or not, God will open or close the doors He desires. So, don't sweat it, God is keeping all the records. If you do not get the credit down here, you will get it up there. If you want to get the credit here, he might allow it. If you don't get the credit, what difference does it make?

Two or three years ago a person said to me, "'So-in-so' is going to take your ministry away from you, he wants to be the one who heads up this ministry." My reply to that statement was "Let him go ahead, I didn't build this ministry anyway. God built it. Let him take it if he can. He will have to take it from God, not me, it belongs to Him. Let God give the ministry and the credit to whoever He desires."

You have, no doubt, heard this saying, "You can have anything you desire if you don't care who gets the credit." My advice to you is that you should go ahead and be obedient to God and enjoy the prosperity He affords and let the other fellow play the grandstands. If he has to have that kind of honor and acclaim to fire his rocket, let him blast off. And know within your own heart that you do not have to indulge in that kind of fraudulent behavior in order to function appropriately for God. You are a spiritual 'basket-case' if you have to have the applause of men to get you turned on and excited about God. There are other, more honorable ways to do it and proper credit can be given by the Lord, wherever and whenever He desires.

I don't think I will surprise you when I make the following statement: It doesn't matter if you are not making headlines in the daily dispatches or if your name is not etched in stone. It doesn't matter! It is indeed a "no, no," in God's economy, for you or I to give credit to ourselves. He would advise you, if it just has to be done, to forget it and let someone else do it. *"Let another man praise thee, and not thine own mouth; a stranger, and not thine own lips"* (Proverbs 27:2).

The Lord's attitude in a matter such as this is something we can learn. Actually, He admitted He could do nothing of Himself. He could only do what He saw His Father do. Whatever the Father is doing, that's exactly what the Son will be doing. Who is getting the credit here? Later He said, *Whenever I pass judgment on something, My judgment is correct, because I seek My Father's will, not Mine* (John 5:19 & 30). He let us know ahead of time who would get the credit. Jesus did not waste His time fretting over who would get the credit.

Chapter 13

You Do Not

Have To Be Irresponsible

Yes, there is hope; you can be the responsible person you have always desired to be. I feel like you desire to take up some slack in your life and be that person that God and others can depend on. It can be done, even though you might think it cannot. Let's look at the situation and see what we can glean to help you become that individual that is trusted by others because they know you are indeed responsible.

Realizing that the Philippians were considerably responsible and obedient, as long as, or while he was with them, Paul challenged them to be that reliable in his absence. Notice how he addressed them concerning their responsibility to God and to the salvation He had entrusted to them.

"...My dear friends, as you have always obeyed me-and that not only when I was with you-now, even more in my absence, complete the salvation that God has given you with a proper sense of awe and responsibility". (Philippians 2:12, Phillips)

Yes, God gave you the salvation you possess in Christ Jesus. It was not something you conjured up in your irresponsible and inconsistent state as an unregenerate person. You were saved by the love, mercy and grace of God, therefore, you need to be a more responsible steward of your salvation. Paul said, *"Complete the salvation"* God was gracious enough to give you. If you are not going to be responsible for the salvation you already possess, who else can do it for you?

The latter part of the above cited verse renders this admonition, *"Work out your own salvation with fear and trembling"* (emphasis mine). Salvation is serious business and it demands the utmost in respect and responsibility to God and man. It is my opinion that if an individual would grow up and be a truly responsible Christian, he would be a responsible person in every area of his life.

The next verse continues to convey the trend of the seriousness of God's love affair with His children. Notice how this relationship is confirmed by God's efforts in the transaction. The apostle said, *"It is God who is at work within you, giving you the will and the power to achieve His purpose"* (v.13). Because of the eternal sanctity of your relationship with Himself, God is perpetually leading and coaching you *in the fine art of Christian responsibility.*

There are some areas in your life where you have shown weakness, and you need to concentrate on strengthening them. Let me list several of these areas and offer some helpful solutions. All of them may not work in your situation, but some will. Work at it, because you need to come to that level of maturity where you can contribute to the welfare of society, rather than being a welfare case yourself. Read on, we will give you some handles to help you become a more responsible, capable, honorable, and reliable Christian individual. You can do it by exerting an extra special amount of will power and God will supply an extra special amount of His grace. *You have no excuse; you can be honorable in everything you do!*

You Can Always Tell The Truth

Yes, just be honest. In His high priestly prayer in John 17, Jesus prayed for His disciples then, every disciple since then, and all His disciples that are alive today. He asked the Father to sanctify (make holy) His disciples, by the truth (v.17). Then He qualified the use of the word 'truth,' by saying to the Father, *"Thy word is truth."* In asking the Father to sanctify us, He was simply petitioning the Father to make us holy. Make them holy by Thy Truth.

The Psalmist confessed, *"Thy word have I hid in my heart that I might not sin against Thee"* (Psalm 119:11). So, my suggestion to you is that you fill your heart with the holy scriptures. The Word of God is the truth and those scriptural truths can make you holy.

In his deep sense of remorse and regret, resulting from his sin of adultery with Bathsheba and from murdering her husband, Uriah, David repented in bitter agony of heart and soul. During his long and rigorous journey back to full communion with God, he acknowledged something sincere Christians should always be aware of. In sincere and earnest confession to God, David admitted to God, *"You desire truth in the inward parts"* (Psalm 51:6). What God desires is exactly what David should have desired and exactly what we must desire, also.

Jesus said, *"I am the Way, the Truth, and the Life"* (John 14:6). Each time you are tempted to misuse the truth, just remember, you will be misusing Jesus.

The Lord, in serious conversation with the Father, actually *'sanctified' Himself for "our sakes."* How? Through the truth (John 17:19). If Jesus was that serious about the truth we should get serious about it also. Amen? Amen!

I desire to counsel you the same way Jesus counseled His disciples then, concerning the truth. He said, *"If you are faithful (keep My Word, Truth) to what I have said, you are truly My disciples. And you will know the truth and the truth will set you free"* (John 8:31 & 32, Phillips, parenthesis mine). Want to be responsible? Catch the little foxes (spirits) that pressure you to lie and cheat. Replace them with the golden nuggets of God's truth. Don't lie to anybody about anything! Be honest in every thought, word, and deed.

You Can Always Be Punctual

There is no legitimate reason for you to be late for every appointment. If you tell your family, your friends, your associates, your peers, your employer or your fellow Christians that you will do something, **DO IT!** If your appointment is at a certain time, *BE THERE! BE THERE ON TIME! Be there ahead of time!*

Look friend, if you are a Christian, your word should be your bond. If you are on program for any kind of an event, and if you arrive 'right on time,' you are thirty minutes late! If everyone else is late, don't take that as an excuse to be late yourself, again; YOU; be there, thirty minutes before! Allow yourself plenty of time for delays. Always being late is one of the little foxes that abort the fruit. Always being late for everything could be demonic and it can spoil many things God desires to accomplish.

Jesus told us about ten bridesmaids who were warned that the Bridegroom was coming. In order to be a part of the ceremonies, they needed lamps for lights to see. They needed oil in their lamps. Five of the ten bridesmaids made themselves ready by making sure they had oil in their lamps. Jesus related the fact that when they were called to go out to meet the bridegroom, five of the bridesmaids failed to be punctual, they were late. They did not prepare or account for delays. The Lord issues to all of us this warning, *"Keep awake and be on the alert, always!"* **"For ye know neither the day nor the hour wherein the Son of Man (Bridegroom) cometh"** (Matthew 25:13). Don't get sidetracked by one of the little foxes that will steal your time and spoil your image.

You Can Be A Disciplined Person

You do not have to be a person that has no stability in your life. Being a disciplined person requires special effort on your part. Your flesh will fight every effort you put forth to add more discipline to your life. But, by the grace of God, you can do it. You will have to make a quality decision and stick to it. Don't think of this as something impossible. The Apostle Paul saw this as a great possibility for those who have made Jesus to be their Lord. He said:

"As you ...have received Christ Jesus the Lord, so walk in Him, having been firmly rooted and now being built up in Him and established in your faith, just as you were instructed..." (Colossians 2:6 & 7, NASB)

What the apostle is doing here is giving us an example of some who had proven the possibility of being established. Hey, if Jesus is your Lord walk it out, He will walk it out with you.

Paul prayed for the Thessalonians too grow up and be established. Notice how sound and solid he prayed for them to be:

"...The Lord make you to increase and abound in love one toward another, toward all men even as we do toward you. To the end He may stablish your hearts unblamable in holiness before God..." (1 Thessalonians 3:12 & 13)

Paul, not only shares the possibility, but the extent to which you can be strengthened and established. But this will not happen automatically, it must be diligently worked at.

The Apostle Peter injects several admonitions that moves one toward being established. Look at these phrases that come as commands: **"Submit yourselves, ...be subject one to another,...be clothed with humility, humble yourselves, cast all your care upon Him,...be sober,... be vigilant, resist the devil steadfastly,... etc. The**

God of all grace, after ye have suffered awhile, make you perfect, stablish, strengthen, settle you" (I Peter 5:5 - 10).

An undisciplined person could never make his way through the rigidity, difficulty and hardship of this type lifestyle. Remember, it can be done.

You Can Always Be Humble

There is no place in the Christian economy for pride. The middle letter in pride is **"I."** The middle letter in sin is **"I."** Too many Christians have **"I"** problems. It is very difficult to see when you have **"I"** problems. If you cannot get healed of your pride you will definitely run into trouble with God. The Bible says, *"God resisteth the proud"* (James 4:6). The root word from which we get the word 'resist' means, among other phrases, *"to range in battle against."*[15] No wonder a haughty spirit precedes a fall. When an individual operates in pride, he declares war against God. The Bible tells us that it is better to be of an humble spirit with the lowly than to divide the spoil with the strong and mighty (Proverbs 16:19). Jesus was always humble.

"Everyone proud and arrogant in heart is disgusting, hateful, and exceedingly offensive to the Lord; be assured [I pledge it] they will not go unpunished." (Proverbs 16:5, Amp.)

The only profitable stance before God is humility. Ministers of the gospel let there be no place in your life and ministry for pride. Parents, at all costs, teach your children to be humble.

You Can Pay Your Honest Debts

Your honor is at stake here. Have you not obligated yourself to meet these commitments? Do you not know that you are under contract to pay these liabilities? If you do not intend to pay for the goods and services you are purchasing, it would be better not to purchase them at all!

Oh, I know, that the 'American Dream' and peer pressure has squeezed you into this insatiable desire for things. You think you just have to have every prestigious thing that others possess. But, it doesn't matter, you do not have to have all these things. And I know that our culture is ever tightening its grip on us as a boa constrictor

44

would continue to squeeze the breath out of its prey. *BUT,* We do not have to be caught up in this kind of exercise! We can say *"NO"* to the pressure and temptation! You say, "Well, I just had to have the money and borrowed on my credit cards to the max." Yes, and you will pay approximately 20%, or more to get it paid back. This debt, along with others will bleed you down to where you cannot provide the real good, wholesome, necessary goods and services your family needs. You cannot give to missions and other charitable things you desire to support. Why? Because you are so strapped down with debts. The Bible says, *"Owe no man any thing, but to love one another: for he that loveth another hath fulfilled the law"* (Romans 13:8).

To be in debt is slavery (Proverbs 22:7). You are bound to your master, the lender. *Being in debt is like being in jail* (Matthew 5:25 & 26). The Bible also says you will not get out of jail until you have paid the last penny. You are not your own, you are bought with the price of your indebtedness and you belong to the power you choose to borrow from. So, pay your debts! You will not be free until you do. Pay up! Don't spend the rest of your life dodging bill-collectors. Be responsible! Stand up and be a real Christian.

You Can Be A Gentleman or Lady

It matters not what women's lib activists think, say or do. There is still a place in this world for women to be ladies and for men to treat them as such. Men may think of themselves as kings, okay, that's good! It makes the ladies queens! They are the queens of our households. Sir, it would not hurt a thing for you to hold the door open for your wife or any other lady.

You can act like a gentleman or a lady when you are in the check-out line, with the cashier or those in line with you. You can do the same thing when your waitress at the restaurant makes a mistake, or when someone in heavy traffic does something you do not think is acceptable. You do not have to act like a _____! You can actually be a Christian lady or gentleman. My religious education teacher in college shared this with our class one day. She said, *"The farther away from God you walk, the more like the beast you become. And the closer to God you walk, the more like Jesus you become."*

45

You Can Clean Up Your Mess

That's right, if you make a mess clean it up! Isn't it sad that you have to follow some adult Christians around and clean up behind them. The task is not too menial for you to clean up your clutter, straighten things out, and put them in order. Leave the situation in the condition you would like to find it in, or leave it in a ***better condition*** than when you received it.

What if you didn't make the mess? Well, you might ought to go ahead and clean it up anyway. This is your world too. You live here along with the rest of us. What do you do when you walk across the floor and find a piece of paper lying there? When you put your garbage in the trash can or dumpster and you miss it with part of your trash, what do you do? Hey, get real, man! Don't expect someone else to clean up your trash! Do it yourself! Who told you that someone else was to baby-sit you and clean up your mess?

You Can Fix It If You Broke It

We all know, 'If it ain't broke, don't fix it!' Just let it alone. But if it is broke, and you are the guilty party, ***fix it! Repair it!*** Especially if it was borrowed, if it belongs to someone else, ***fix it!*** You need to be more than a demolition agent, if you profess to be a Christian. You need to be a repairer of the breach (Isaiah 58:12). Don't break hearts, fix them!

You Can Refrain From The Use of Profanity

You do not have the time nor the breath to spend or waste on cursing. What's going on inside your brain that causes your mouth to unload such garbage? Some people have things in their mouths that I wouldn't have in my hands. What is in your brain that comes rolling out so freely? I think a better question to ask is, "What is not in your brain?" What is lacking that causes you to have to improvise and substitute for good wholesome words? You probably need to go back to school and improve your vocabulary so you will not be so poverty stricken when you need to talk. If all you have to offer when you open your mouth is profanity and vulgarity, you need to keep your mouth shut! That kind of noise pollution does not need to be spoken in the presence of men, much less in the presence of women and children.

The Bible tells us that out of the abundance of the heart the mouth speaks (Luke 6:45). Really, it's out of the 'overflow' of the heart that the mouth erupts with such nonsense. When you use such language, what have you done that will be helpful to anyone? You have been told to keep your tongue from evil and your lips from speaking guile (Psalms 34:13). So, be a responsible Christian, and not one that has such a small vocabulary and cannot control his tongue.

He talked with a real southern drawl and never allowed his emotions to overtake him. My friend and colleague in the ministry, was well respected as a man of much wisdom and integrity, as well as a competent minister of the gospel. The southern drawl, which characterized his conversation, was very slow in coming forth. When he opened his mouth he gradually released his words with much caution. Not only was he extremely slow in what he finally said, there were blanks and extended spaces of silence in his sentences. After church one Sunday, someone asked him, "Why do you talk so slow? Why does it take you so long to speak so few words." His belated answer was, "Before I was converted, I worked in a blacksmith shop. There, it was very easy for a sinner to find occasions to unload his mind by cursing and using profanity. After I was converted to Jesus, I had to leave out all my choice adjectives and four letter words. It takes a while for me to re-structure my sentences and some times I just have to skip over some of those unnecessary words." It might be good for you to leave out some of your favorite adjectives and other four-letter words and re-structure your sentences to convey wholesome communication.

You Can Be Thorough In Every Transaction

Don't do a poor job at anything you do. Give it your best attention. Remember who you are! Also, remember *Whose* you are. You are not your own, you are bought with a price. You owe it to yourself, to the Christian faith, and to the Lord Jesus Christ, to do your very best. *Your policy should contain a standard of excellence known as 'perfection,'* as a goal to shoot for, in your every undertaking. Many people are watching you simply because you are a Christian. If you dropped it, pick it up! If you started it, finish it!

You Can Return That which Is Borrowed

I cannot for the life of me understand where the unspoken idea of *'If I borrow it, it becomes mine,'* originated. If you have borrowed it, it is not yours. What you have borrowed is someone else's property. Again, it is not yours, take it back to its rightful owner. I don't know if failing to return that which is borrowed, is stealing or armed robbery. Either way, it is taking something that is not your own. Be sure to wake up in this area of your life and become a responsible person. Remember, you profess to be a Christian.

You Can Be A Good Steward

A steward is a manager or a trustee. He is one that oversees certain estates, properties, etc. A steward is not the owner, he is one that is entrusted with the owner's property. This steward is one who can arrange things and put them in order. He is to be responsible for all he oversees. One part of his responsibility is to maintain the property and keep it in a good state of repair. Another responsibility is that he improves the property and is to leave it in a much better condition than when he started. To do so he must make sure that *every aspect* of his responsibility is duly cared for and improved. Remember this, you must be a good steward of everything God has entrusted into your care. *Can He trust you to handle His affairs?*

Be a good steward of your time. Time is very fragile, treat it with care. Treat it with prayer. Make every moment count! The Psalmist prayed and asked God to teach us to number or count our days so that we might gain or give unto Him a heart of wisdom (Psalm 90:12). Paul admonished us to redeem the time because the days are evil (Ephesians 5:16). As a good steward of Jesus Christ, be sure to guard against wasting your valuable time. Make every moment count for God and for eternity!

You can be a good steward of your money. Don't waste it on trivial things. Make it count also. Your money needs to count for God. It needs to count for the welfare of your family. Make it count for your child's salvation, health, education, and true welfare. As mentioned earlier, stay out of debt in order to keep from wasting it on high interest. *"Give, and it shall be given unto you"* (Luke 6:38). Your financial advisor will tell you how to invest for the future. If you give for the cause of Christ you will be investing in kingdom giving and kingdom living, plus laying up treasures in heaven.

You can be a good steward of your body. You have only one body, take care of it! It is the dwelling place of God, *keep it clean!* Your body can easily be neglected, *don't do it!* It can be exposed to things that will destroy it like: extreme heat or cold, alcohol or drugs, tobacco, fatigue, lack of exercise, bad food, disease, physical abuse, all kinds of sin, etc., *protect it!*

When you begin to get older and the body begins to wear out, you will see the importance of taking care of it. While you are young is a good time to start being a good steward of your body.

And by the way, make it more pleasing to look at. Again, you are a Christian and you need to look like one. There is no reason why you should have to dress so slouchy and sloppy. I am not saying you have to dress formal, but you do need to look decent. What I am really saying is for you to be clean in your body and in your dress, and look like a Christian. You can also brush your teeth to keep from being offensive to others, and comb your hair for the same reason. It will not hurt a thing if you do a better job of personal grooming and hygiene. Who is pressuring you to look like you just pulled your clothes out of a rag bag. If you are a Christian, represent Him in the best possible way.

You can be a good steward of your mind. Take care of it also. It will last you a long time, especially if you take good care of it. It needs to be used. It needs to be fed. It needs to be educated. It needs to relax, because it gets tired. Your mind needs to be renewed. The Bible tells us that we can be transformed by the renewing of our minds (Romans 12:2). Mind renewal helps us know the will of God. Renewing the mind comes by feeding it on the Word of God. The Word of God is the will of God and to saturate the mind with the Word of God helps us to know and recognize the will of God. I believe the Word of God can also heal the mind of man. So, be sure to keep it clean! Get the garbage out and the Word of God in.

Do good, heavy, spiritual warfare and follow the admonition of the Apostle Paul to the Corinthians and "Bring every thought captive to the obedience of Christ" (II Corinthians 10:5).

You can be a good steward of your home. Clean it up for the sake of your family, friends, visitors, and for good health reasons. ***Keep it clean*** for the same reasons! A clean house is a good and proper witness for Jesus Christ. When people come into your home, will they smell an odor that testifies to the fact that you have neglected the place God has provided for you and HE to dwell? Every family needs to be a responsible Christian in this area of the stewardship of their home.

Lady of the house, or whoever is responsible, keep your spouse's clothes neat and clean and presentable in public. Like your children, he represents the stewardship of your household. If he is a public figure, how can you sit when he stands before people, untidy, looking like he has slept in his clothes? I know, He's a grown man and should be a responsible person himself. But, who is responsible for his clothes being clean and tidy?

You can be a good steward of your work. What kind of work do you do? No, I do not desire to know what you do for a living, your trade, your job classification, or your profession. My desire is to know ***how well*** you do in ***everything*** you do. If it is worth doing, it's worth doing right. Are you a workman that needeth not to be ashamed? More later on this.

Be sure to be a good witness for Jesus by being industrious. Don't be lazy! Work! Good, old fashion work will not hurt you. Earn your bread by the sweat of your brow! Pay your own way, work for a living! Don't expect anyone to pick up the tab for you. There are no free lunches. Somebody will have to pay for them, somehow, someday. Don't try to get something for nothing! Every time you try to get something for nothing, you lose.

The Apostle Paul had to deal with slothful people as he ministered. He spoke directly to the situation with these words to the church at Thessalonica:

> ***"When we were... with you we gave you this principle to work on: 'If a man will not work, he shall not eat.' Now we hear that you have some among you living quite undisciplined lives, never doing a stroke of work, and busy only in other people's affairs. Our order to such men, indeed our appeal by the Lord Jesus Christ, is to settle down to work and eat the food they have earned themselves.***

50

And the rest of you, my brothers - don't get tired of honest work! If anyone refuses to obey the command given in this letter, mark that man; do not associate with him until he is ashamed of himself. I don't mean, of course, treat him as an enemy, but reprimand as a brother." (II Thessalonians 3:10 - 15, Phillips)

I feel sure Paul was attempting to show that *slothfulness is a curse* and that *work is a virtue.*

Now, back to good workmanship. In your work, do the best job you possibly can. Do quality work always. *The best way to be a Christian on the job is to give your employer the best day's work you possibly can.* Keep your standards high and allow the quality of your work to be an excellent and vibrant witness for Jesus.

Solomon said this about a lazy person: *"He becomes poor who works with a slack and idle hand, but the hand of the diligent makes rich"* (Proverbs 10:4, Amp.).

You can be a good steward of your children. When people see your children they automatically think of you. Their comparison and evaluation may not always be correct, but you are the one they think of. When you take them into public make sure they are clean and dressed well. Don't allow them to be little *'Tasmanian devils'* that destroy yours and other people's property. Some children have the privilege to play *'Demolition Derby,'* while their parents observe and cheer them on from the sidelines. Some parents say, *"My children don't bother me, I just tune them out."* For God's sake, *don't tune them out while they are being disobedient and destructive!* Teach them to have respect for other people and especially their elders.

Parents, are your children those who have to wait for you to pick them up late at night? Are they waiting at the theater, skating rink, ball game, etc., unsupervised and unprotected, with nothing to do but get into trouble or get hurt? Are you a parent who does not know where your children are in the late hours of the night? What about during school hours, are you sure they are at school?

They are your kids, and you definitely need to know their whereabouts. As long as they are under your roof you are liable. You are responsible for them!

So, train up your child in the way that he should go (Proverbs 22:6). You owe it to your children to discipline them in a Godly manner. Give them the best training possible by bringing them up in the nurture and admonition of the Lord. Undisciplined children become rebels in the home, and afterward, they are rebels at school, on the street, on the job, in the military, and even in jail. Do all you can to teach them to be humble and to have the utmost respect for authority. Undisciplined children in the homes today are potential outlaws on the streets tomorrow. Take some good advice and discipline your children, in a special effort to prevent creating a monster that could turn on you and devour you.

Many times parents tend to allow their children to do whatever they wish. They try to give them whatever their little heart's desire. This is very dangerous. It seems that there is an unwritten law floating around that says, "Whatever the child wants, he must have it." The child demands it and the parents, etc., are driven by some kind of unseen force to obey the commands of the child when he makes such demands on the parents.

Many times children throw fits of temper as a lever to pressure parents into granting them what they want. Some parents, because they have been relaxed in their discipline earlier, have difficulty stopping these fits of anger. They do not know how to handle it. The best thing to do is not allow it from the very beginning. These kids do what we call 'throwing a fit.' My wife and I raised four children and helped with several others. I have never seen a child yet, that could throw a bigger fit than I can. Parents, let me ask you this question: ***"Are your children the tail that wags the dog?"***

Maybe we should look at some of the things God has to say about the disciplining of children.

"Foolishness is bound in the heart of a child; but the rod of correction will drive it far from him." (Proverbs 22:15)

"Withhold not correction from the child: for if thou beatest him with the rod, he shall not die." (Proverbs 23:13)

"Thou shalt beat him with the rod, and shalt deliver his soul from hell." (Proverbs 23:14)

"The blueness of a wound cleanseth away evil: so do stripes the inward parts of the belly" (Proverbs 20:30). The

Amplified Version states this verse, thusly: *"**Blows that wound cleanse away evil, and strokes [for correction] reach the innermost parts.**"*

*"**And ye fathers, provoke not your children to wrath: but nurture them in the chastening and admonition of the Lord.**"* (Ephesians 6:4)

Paul gives pertinent instruction to Timothy on the qualifications of a bishop. One of the specifications has to do with raising one's children.

The bishop should be one who rules his house well, and keeps *"**His children under control, with true dignity, commanding their respect in every way and keeping them respectful. For if a man does not know how to rule his own household, how is he to take care of the church of God?**"* (I Timothy 3:4 & 5, Amp.). With reference to the word 'gravity' (used in verse 4 by the KJV), W. E. Vine says this is "A necessary characteristic of the teaching imparted by a servant of God."[16] Vine is simply attempting to share with us the importance of child discipline.

This does not mean that only church leaders should discipline their children. All parents should bring their children up in the nurture and admonition and chastening of the Lord. The conduct of a bishop's children (or those of any church leader) determines whether or not he can manage the church effectively.

Parents, please, take special note of your children. Satan is out to destroy them. If we do not stand in the gap for our children we will loose them. We have nearly lost an entire generation of kids because of sinister and malignant attitudes and practices in our homes, schools, government and the laxity in law enforcement. Rise up, O men of God, do something for this and the next generation of children. Constant, heavy warfare needs to be fought in the heavenlies on behalf of our precious, God-given children. Notice what Solomon had to say about failing to take disciplinary action, anywhere:

*"**BECAUSE SENTENCE AGAINST AN EVIL WORK IS NOT EXECUTED SPEEDILY, THEREFORE THE HEART OF THE SONS OF MEN IS FULLY SET IN THEM TO DO EVIL**"* (Ecclesiastes 8:11)

Your children are an outgrowth of yourself, so, as far as in you lies, train them to be what you desire for them to be. Our children are the greatest single natural resource that we can bequeath to the next generation. Lets give them our best.

You can be a good steward of your ministry. This is serious business. I don't know who you are and neither do I know what you do for a living. I am not aware of your gifts, graces, or your calling. This, I do know, you need to be a good steward of those things listed immediately above. They were given to you by God Himself. Paul said, ***"The gifts and callings of God are without repentance"*** (Romans 11:29). More simply put, ***"The gifts and callings of God are irrevocable"*** (Amp.). Vine says the Greek word from which we get our word *'repentance,'* signifies that it is *"Without change of purpose.*[17] The word in this case is an adjective, whereas the verb means 'a change of mind or purpose.' God does not say, "If you don't like it I will take it back." You possess these gifts and you will keep them for a while. Make sure you use them specifically for God's purposes.

PAUL'S METHOD FOR A MIGHTY MINISTRY (II Corinthians 6:3 - 10, NASB). Notice his attitude and demeanor concerning his ministry.

He was sensitive about the witness of his ministry.

Paul was careful not to discredit the ministry God had put him into. He gave *"No cause for offense in anything, in order that the ministry be not discredited."*

He conducted himself as a servant.

He said in everything we *"Commend ourselves as servants of God..."*

He learned and exhibited perseverance.

He was making a point for us as he shared the many hardships he had endured. We are not exempt from any of these trials and tribulations ourselves (vs. 4 & 5).

He proved the ministry to be one of integrity.

His ministry was conducted ***"In purity, in knowledge, in patience, in kindness..."*** (v.6).

He employed the use of Christian graces and power in his ministry.

"...In the Holy Spirit, in genuine love, in the Word of truth, in the power of God; by the weapons of righteousness..." (vv. 6 & 7).

He weathered every storm of persecution and heartbreak.

"...By glory and dishonor, by evil report and good report, regarded as deceivers and yet true, as unknown yet well known, as dying yet behold, we live; as punished yet not put to death, as sorrowful yet always rejoicing, as poor yet making many rich, as having nothing yet possessing all things" (vv. 8, 9, & 10). In a teaching entitled, *"10 "M"s For True Ministers,"* Dr. Bill Hamon, of Christian International, Point Washington, Florida, said, *"GOD MAKES A MAN BEFORE MANIFESTING MIGHTY MINISTRY."*

God never intended to leave His sheep unattended. He never intended to leave His sheep with a hireling. Sad to say, many people who call themselves servants of God are hirelings. Since they are in it for ulterior, undisclosed purposes, the wolves come in and scatter the sheep (See John 10:12 & 13).

"Unlike so many, we do not peddle the Word of God for profit. On the contrary, in Christ we speak before God with sincerity, LIKE MEN SENT FROM GOD." (II Corinthians 2:17, NIV)

Don't say you cannot do a good job, God gifted you to do it. Be a good steward of what God has entrusted you with and is expecting you to do. You are playing with jagged lightening bolts when you fool around in this area of your life.

Stop playing ministry!

Either get it right and get in or get out!

You can indeed be a responsible person. Everything you need to do to be responsible is written in the Bible. Study it and learn for yourself. You do not have to take my word for it. *Pray for God to give you a heart that loves Him and that desires to be like Him.*

Chapter 14

You Do Not

Have To Broadcast Your Success

Who is going to grant you an extra set of brownie points if you wave your scorecard where all can see? You do not need to exhibit your successful ventures in the face of others. God will acknowledge your trophies **through** others, therefore, you will not have to go to the trouble to advertise your accomplishments yourself. It is so easy for some Christians, and especially preachers, to strut their achievements with great swelling words and awe-inspiring adjectives when it is so unnecessary. Its really easier not to. The results will be worse, especially if you are so bent on making an explosive report. This kind of dishonest activity can cause your fruit to be contaminated (see Chapter 5). Why? Because you were not studying to show yourself approved unto God, you were seeking man's approval. When a workman rightly divides the word of truth he does not need to be ashamed (II Timothy 2:15). Therefore, he will not have to broadcast his success and give an inflated report. Jesus never made glowing reports to advertise His accomplishments.

He even cautioned His disciples to do likewise. He said to them and to us, *"Believe Me for the very works sake"* (John 14:11). That's what will count, the works, and not some exaggerated success story. *"For men to search their own glory is not glory"* (Proverbs 25:27). Let go and let.God do it His way. He knows exactly what needs to be done and exactly how to get it accomplished, and if He needs to go public with it, He can handle it without our help.

Jesus sent out a short-term team of seventy missionaries to divide up in teams of two and minister to a harvest that was great (Luke 10:1 & 2). They were under authority because they were sent by Jesus. They were given authority and power over demons (v.19). Because they were sent, and because they were obedient, and because they were anointed; they were indeed successful. God truly honors His word! Like many people today, this team came back waving their banners, blasting their trumpets and parading their grand achievements. Jesus immediately saw through their merchandising and broadcasting tactics and showed them four things that needed to be brought to their attention:

He said, *"I saw Satan falling as fast as lightening…,"* meaning, *"Your Fifth Avenue approaches to Kingdom advancement will fall flat on its face, soon"* (v.18).

"It is I Who gives you this kind of authority and anointing, if there is any success in this venture, it is Mine. Leave the success stories off. *If I have to, I'll write another set of scriptures, to get everything reported correctly."*

"And too, I have protected you, I told you nothing would hurt you. You should be thankful that you lived to tell about it" (v.19).

"But don't rejoice in all this 'success.' If you are going to shout about anything, Praise God for the fact that your names are written in Heaven"* (v.20). Their problem was that they were strutting about, saying, "Whew, what a heavy anointing I had on me!" **That is extremely unnecessary! Listen friend, your reputation has preceded and introduced you. Whether real or imagined, the anointing speaks for itself, you will not have to toot your own whistle.**

The individual that attempts to flaunt and exhibit his triumphs to the people in the grandstands will not impress God in the least. And furthermore, when he is "tooting his own horn," he is submitting a counterfeit, distorted and perverted report. God is not interested in our success or our success stories. These inflated ego explosions will not bless nor impress people that are truly sensitive to the Holy Spirit. I think the individual who plays the grandstands should try giving a little praise, honor and glory to God. O Yes, remember this, that the people in the grandstands are not as easily conned as you might assume. They are tired of hearing the falsified reports many are giving about how many thousands were saved because of your *"great anointing and spiritual expertise."*

You do not have to make such a glowing report. God is the One who is keeping the record that will count for eternity. For God's sake, don't let the devil make your report for you. He will botch it up every time. It will look good, sound good, and may even make the headlines. But, it will stink! Make your report yourself and be honest. Satan will use your voice box or speech mechanism to misrepresent your own case. It is much easier to simply be honest. Is our reward in heaven or are we so desperate that we resort to telling tall tales so we can go ahead and cash in our heavenly rewards here, and now, and bankrupt our eternity?

"Lay not up for yourselves treasures upon earth where moths and rust doth corrupt, and where thieves break through and steal: but lay up for yourselves treasures in heaven, where neither moth nor rust doth corrupt, and where thieves do not break through nor steal: for where your treasure is there will your heart be also." (Matthew 6:19 - 21)

Recently, I was listening to Dr. James Dobson on his radio broadcast, *'Focus on the Family.'* He made a statement that caught my attention, and speaks directly to our situation here. He said, "If you live long enough, the world will crash your trophies." What Dobson was attempting to convey was this: After we have climbed the ladder of success and have accomplished the many, many things that have brought us to where we are, who will remember them? It will be like that phrase in Lincoln's famous "Gettysburg Address:" "The world will little note nor long remember what we said here..." All that will be remembered and all that we accomplish, will be only that which is eternal. Our successes here are only temporal, but what God accomplishes through us will live on, eternally. So, our accomplishments will die and therefore are not worth publishing.

Is your reward in heaven, or, are you in such desperate straits that you have just got to pull it off down here? Go ahead, push it to the max, milk it for everything its worth, if that's your desire. Just remember this...God will not sanction it.

Remember, you are not performers... you are Ministers!

Chapter 15

You Do Not

Have To Protect Your Reputation

What kind of reputation do you have anyway? This is a wonderful place for us to call for servitude. Why? What does servitude have to do with reputation? Well, it really doesn't matter how I think these two words relate, but it does make a difference in how Jesus appraised them. The Apostle Paul advised us to have the same mind in us that Jesus had in Himself (see Philippians 2:5 - 8). Jesus was (is) indeed God. This is one of the strongest assertions in the New Testament of the Deity of our Savior. This passage does not teach that Jesus emptied Himself of His divine nature or His attributes. He only emptied Himself of the outward manifestations of the Godhead. God never ceases to be God. Jesus never made a great deal of the fact that He was equal with God. He didn't 'flip out' over the equality. He didn't get overly enthusiastic about trying to grasp it or to retain it. He didn't build up a good head of steam or get bent all out of shape about His Deity. Paul said that Jesus:

"Made himself of no reputation, and took upon him the form of a servant..." (Philippians 2:7)

The word used here for "reputation," in the Greek is 'KENOO.' It literally means: *"to make empty, to abase, neutralize, to make of none affect, void, vain,"* (Strong's & Vines). This is what Jesus thought about "His" reputation. There are several correct renderings of this word and passage: *"He emptied Himself,"* or *"This is a graphic expression of the completeness of His self-renunciation,"*[18] or *"He divested Himself of His visible glory"* (The New Schoefield Reference Bible, column reference). Please notice the connection to Isaiah 53:12, *"He poured out His soul unto death."* It looks like the Prophet Isaiah and the Apostle Paul have been reading the same books. Evidently, Jesus kept pouring out until the vessel was empty.

The person that protects and promotes his reputation is relying on his 'rep' instead of relying on God. **JESUS RELINQUISHED HIS REPUTATION IN ORDER TO BE A SERVANT OF THE MOST HIGH GOD.** For y(our) sake(s).

We are not talking about damaging or spoiling the image of God, we must protect that at all costs. We are dealing with the fact that some Christian individuals are trying to work out their salvation **WITHOUT** fear and trembling.

All Christians are to assume responsibility for the reputation of God and His Church, of which Jesus is the Head. It is ***His reputation*** that we are undertaking to protect, not ours. We must follow in the steps of Jesus, Who had a much greater reputation than ours. He abandoned His great 'rep' and became a servant, obedient unto death, the death of the cross. And that cross bought your salvation and mine, the greatest success story ever told. This was accomplished by Jesus, not us. The reason many people today cannot reach their goal, or whatever God desires for their lives, is because ***they are depending on their 'impeccable' reputation, rather than the death and resurrection of the Sinless Son of God.***

Since it is His Name and image and witness we are to gain and maintain, we need to acquire the same mind and attitude of our Lord (Philippians 2:5). We need to allow our lights to shine in order to glorify our Father (Matthew 5:16).

Protecting and promoting your reputation can keep you from being the **SERVANT** you need to be, from being as **HUMBLE** as you need to be, and from being as **OBEDIENT** (unto death) as you need to, and from **EMPTYING** yourself as much as you need to. Do you really and truly desire to live for Jesus? How strong is that desire to live for Him? These activities and characteristics that are highlighted in this section (also listed in vv. 7 & 8 of Philippians 2) should cast heavy challenges upon us. Again, how strong is that desire to live for Him? What is your estimation of His worth? Is Jesus worth living for? Is He worth dying for? His estimation of you was such that He believed you were worth dying for.

This little fox, of *"Protecting Our Reputation"* is remarkably shrewd and must be watched carefully. The reason he is so sly is because *'Protecting Your Rep'* sounds like a good thing to do. Therefore, we must be extremely cautious to keep it from spoiling our desire to be like Jesus.

When we arrive at the place where we are willing to die for Him we will not be so anxious about our own reputations, but will be diligently promoting and protecting His.

Chapter 16

You Do Not

Have To Be Entertained

The true Christian life is NOT boring. The poet said, "Every day with Jesus is sweeter than the day before." Every day in the life of a dedicated Christian is a brand new adventure. Your life does not have to be monotonous. There is no reason for you to have to be looking for something to do to keep you from being weary from inactivity. Be sure to make every attempt to keep some spiritual mentor from having to constantly baby-sit you. Really, you do not have to be entertained.

Let me share a few things that will keep you from being bored by the silence and/or inactivity, something that can prove to you that you do not need to be entertained.

Praying is one of the most exciting things you can do! Try it, you will like it. And besides, you will be talking to your Creator. He truly knows how to speak what you need to hear. Listen up!

And, too, you can think on good things, not on the evening news, nor the stock market, nor the liberal media, nor the sports news, nor the latest gossip, nor the political debates, but you can think on good things, Godly things, wholesome things, Holy things, and positive things. Paul gives a list of these "good things" in Philippians 4:8, and suggests that we think about them. Turn to it right now and read them and start saying and thinking on them.

The Apostle preceded this list by telling his readers: "The peace of God which passes all understanding, shall keep your hearts and minds through Christ Jesus." Take it from me, *"You do not have to be entertained."* God will do it through Christ but you have to be corrected and connected.

Helping other people will also be a great substitute for the person who thinks he has to turn on the radio or television or go to a ball game to keep from 'going stark, raving mad.' If you have to rely on these things to navigate and function well, you are truly missing some of the activity that is always better than the things this world has to offer. Why don't you try doing helpful things for the elderly, or helping feed and clothe the poor, or going to a prayer meeting, or witnessing to a lost soul about Jesus. What about visiting that lonely individual who sets for hours waiting, hoping for someone to drop by just to say "Hello, how are you doing today?" The world cannot afford these eternal luxuries. It would bankrupt Wall Street to do what the Body of Christ can do.

Above, we referred to a list of **THINGS** in Philippians 4:8 to think about. Now, we are suggesting **SOMEONE** to think about. Read the following verse and learn what the prophet Isaiah said God would do for the individual who keeps his mind on God.

"You will guard him and keep him in perfect and constant peace whose mind (both its inclination and its character) is stayed on You, because he commits himself to You, leans on You, and hopes confidently in you." (Isaiah 26:3, Amp.)

Many years ago as a young pastor an elderly Christian gentleman said to me, *"It always does a person good to allow the Name of Jesus to flow through his mind every moment of the day."* Try it! Every time you think about it, just say, *"Jesus, Jesus, Jesus!"*

The writer of Hebrews offers this word of counsel: *"Let your ambition be to live at peace with all men and to achieve holiness without which no man shall see the Lord"* (Hebrews 12:14, Phillips). He is simply saying that we should strive to live at peace and live a holy life. Again, the world cannot even come close to competing with that.

Many things today, such as campaigns, camp-meetings, seminars, revivals, etc., go under the guise of kingdom advancement and evangelism. These things were paramount to most people in the crowds that followed Jesus. They followed Him for the sensual pleasure of seeing the miracles. To them these assemblies were no more than some kind of "spiritual" entertainment, which hopefully would hold them until the next one came along. These emotional 'highs' were not strong enough to sustain and support them when the pressure began to rise. So, they had to be entertained. It is indeed sad that many things that are done in the Name of Jesus are only entertainment. This is not an attempt to satirize the genuine, but if the shoe fits, put it on and wear it until proper correction is made. Be sure to allow the Holy Spirit to be your coach in the correction process.

If you are bored you are not at peace. You need something to entertain you, something to sustain you, something to occupy your mind, something to prop you up while you are in this irrational state. You need a sedative, something to calm your nerves. The thing you are looking for is "peace." In the Hebrew, the word is "SHALOM" and primarily means ***"wholeness, full, finished and made perfect."*** The verb, ***"follow"*** (Hebrews 12:14, KJV) is used in most translations, but, Phillips uses the word, "achieve." Marvin Vincent says the verb *'is used of the pursuit of moral and spiritual ends."*[19] If you are on the stretch for God, ***you need to speed on swiftly, in hot pursuit of His holiness.*** In I Thessalonians 5:23, Paul sends this prayer up for us:

"...May the God of peace Himself sanctify you through and through (separate you from profane things, make you pure and wholly consecrated to God); and may your spirit and soul and body be preserved sound and complete (and found) blameless at the coming of our Lord Jesus Christ (the Messiah)." (Amp.)

The phrase ***"through and through"*** (Amp.) is a correlation of the same Greek word for "ENTIRE" or "WHOLLY," in earlier versions. And it means ***"complete, sound in every part,"*** and is used ethically in this verse. It ***"indicates that every grace present in Christ should be manifested in the believer."***[20]

The presence of boredom and monotony signifies a lack or an emptiness of some kind. The scriptures that we are dealing with here are speaking of "WHOLENESS," especially as it relates to Jesus. Can you picture Jesus having to go to a movie, or listen to the warped media present their version of the 6:00 O'clock News, or having to drive several hundred miles to see a 'favorite team' play some kind of ball game, or having to step outside to smoke, or having to rent a video, or taking a "toddy for the body," or . ..whatever crutch he might have addicted himself to? If we possess "every grace present in Christ" we will not need all these substitutes and counterfeits that so many people are running themselves ragged to receive. No, you don't have to "go nuts," you can go with God. If we make it our primary purpose and a priority item to ***"seek the kingdom of God and His righteousness,"*** God will add the things to us that we desire. Having to be entertained is another 'little fox' that is spoiling our vines. You are a dead drag or drain on the Kingdom of God if we have to keep baby sitting you.

Needing to be entertained is a serious sign of a vacancy or a void in the inner life. Jesus said we would have life abundantly-implying that He would fill it. Christians mistake the 'need' for entertainment as a need for relationship or fellowship. Through the word of God, Jesus provides every possible answer to what we need. It comes in the form of our salvation, our relationship TO HIM, our place IN HIM, and our position as part of His Body. That is why the New Testament Church met regularly; to have abundance in Jesus through BODY LIFE! *The Body, fitly joined together (Ephesians 4:16) meets every need.* It is my observation that, if an individual would become absorbed in the Body of believers, God would do a marvelous job of entertaining him. Jesus can do a better job of satisfying you than any entertainer I know.

Chapter 17

You Do Not

Have To Be 'Super' Spiritual

I always feel a special need to minister to people who are continually trying to exhibit their 'spiritual' prowess and intimacy to God by loud, verbal and "spiritual" expressions. Their futile attempts to demonstrate their spirituality is sometimes presented in irresponsible physical gestures and sometimes by religious facial expressions. If this kind of pious conduct is mistaken for spirituality, the devil has done a good job of manipulation on that individual. If you have bought this bill of goods from Satan you truly need to realize that you 'have been had.' To repeatedly shout "Praise the Lord" and "Hallelujah" is in no way a proof of how spiritual you are.

It will in no way make you more intimate with Jesus. Neither will it grant you any 'spiritual merit badges.' This type of hype brings absolutely no special anointing. It doesn't put you on God's honor roll. It will not put you in a position to receive any bonus points in your faith walk.

Down under all that facade of *'super-spirituality,'* there is an un-repented sin, an emptiness, a hurt, a foreign spirit, etc. that craves attention and recognition. It tries to compensate by loud 'spiritual' talk and overt, physical, erratic behavior. Another way to compensate for these inadequacies is to be extremely bold about what they think they are hearing from God. They are boisterous in saying, *"God told me!"* In their immaturity they really and truly do not know that they are operating out of their immature emotions, and because of that the Devil sells them a bill of goods. They can do damage to themselves and others when they learn that *God did NOT tell them.* These 'youngsters' are honest when they say such things and they think they are 'more' spiritual because of it. I like Dr. Bill Hamon's counsel in training young Christians in prophetic ministry, he tells them to say, *'I think'* or *'I feel like'* or *'I believe'* this is what God is saying."

In no way, I repeat, in no way, am I taking or making an underhanded punch at sincere shouting, singing, praising, dancing in the spirit for our Lord. But, I am coming against hollow, empty, overt expressions and physical gestures that only inflate the human ego. If these expressions are not real, if they have not been bathed and baptized in earnest, heart-felt, sincere prayer, they are not of God and will do great harm to kingdom advancement. Great harm to that lost person who is observing from the sidelines, and to young Christians who are being impressed by these charlatans.

In many instances this type of conduct is presented and promoted by older Christians, and therefore, teaches younger ones that this is normal Christianity. No, it is not 'normal' Christianity! It is an abnormal or a sub-normal species that causes others to become *"Charlatan Christians."* It may take several years for them to discover that 'super-spiritual' behavior is a strong advocate of hypocrisy.

Earlier, when I said, I feel the need to minister to these unfortunate people, it is because I know there is a dangerous problem inside that needs critical care immediately. When I am in the presence of an individual who is exhibiting his little sanctified ritual, trying to impress me as to his 'spiritual' achievements, I just listen. I dare not allow the devil to intimidate me by lying and trying to convince me that my spiritual temperature is too low. The main thing on the agenda at that moment is to learn from the Holy Spirit how I can minister to this person. He is having to work overtime carrying this extra load of the devil's merchandise. My heart reaches out to him, desiring to help him find his healing. He is in desperate need of the Great Physician.

If you feel you have to personally and purposely demonstrate your spirituality, your holiness, your dedication, your anointing—You desperately need to go back to the altar and check it out with God to be sure you still possess all the above.

"Like clouds and wind without rain is a man who boasts of his gifts falsely." (Proverbs 25:14, NASB)

Some of the best scriptures that expose this type demeanor are listed in Chapter I on **"You Do Not Have To Tell Everything You Know."** Many times it is "that little unruly member" in your mouth, called the tongue, that is used of the devil to make these kinds of unnecessary exhibitions. In most cases it is the tongue that betrays the innate hypocrisy of the heart.

Chapter 18

You Do Not

Have To Push Your Agenda

A careful study of the earthly existence of Jesus will reveal the fact that He did not push His Personal agenda. I feel sure that Jesus was setting an example for us to imitate. Sure, He had many things to accomplish, but those were the things on God's agenda. He said, *"I must work the works of Him that sent Me, while it is day; the night cometh, when no man can work"* (John 9:4). Oh yes, He had a schedule, and the clock and the calendar were progressively moving toward a deadline. Night was closing in fast. Many things needed to be accomplished. The fields were white unto harvest, but the laborers were few. Being the Lord of the harvest Himself, He could see all the more reason to truly get on schedule. The work that He came to do was not His own, it was the works of the Father.

Even though Jesus saw the fields that were white unto harvest, He saw something more important. Let's see if we can see what He saw.

"I tell you the truth, the Son of man can do nothing by Himself; He can only do what He sees the Father doing, because whatever the Father does the Son also does." (John 5:19,NIV)

We can notice from the Lord's own words that He was not promoting His own program. He was saying, as it were, **"I ONLY DO WHAT I SEE MY FATHER DOING."** He gazed over the City of Jerusalem and wept because of her sin. At this moment, He could have become emotional enough to call ten leagues of angels to rescue the city from her plight. O yes, He saw the city, steeped in sin and debauchery, but He saw His Father in sharper focus. Jesus looked upon the multitudes and was moved with compassion. Why didn't He do something? He did! Yes, He did exactly what He saw His Father doing. And *He did only what He saw the Father do.*

John records another episode where Jesus refused to push His own agenda. Jesus said:

"I can of mine own self do nothing. As I hear, I judge, and My judgment is just, because I seek not mine own will, but the will of the Father that sent Me." (John 5:30)

He spoke very plainly here and simply said, "I am not looking to find My own will (plan, program or agenda), I am attempting to see and do what My Father is doing. The Master is giving us some good, solid and sound advice in letting us know why His judgment is right. Why? **Because He sought the Father's will in every circumstance.**

The Gospels are replete with the facts to prove that Jesus was not promoting His own program. Let's look at another one. *He did only what the Father had taught Him* (John 8:28). And in the next verse He approves the Father's agenda by letting us know that *He always does those things that pleases the Father.*

When you push and promote your program, you are going to wreak havoc in the plans and programs God is working in the lives of other individuals who love Him and are trying to do His will. **If it is your little program**, do the rest of us a favor, and trash it! But, if it is:

What you see God doing, go for it!

God's will, go for it!

What He has taught you, go for it!

Pleasing to the Father; go for it!

If we do it His way many people will be blessed and lifted. Let's not push our agendas, *they will not work!* Isn't it refreshing sometimes to find someone who doesn't have an agenda of their own to unload and explode on everyone else.

Chapter 19

You Do Not

Have To Be A Chronic Complainer

Yes, I know, you have had a bad time, all your life. You had an unhappy childhood. You were stricken by an incurable disease. You were jilted at the altar. You lost a fortune in the stock market. You had a 'run-in' with an individual at the church. You were defeated in your bid for public office. You didn't have the opportunity to complete your education. So-in-so doesn't like you. That other individual did not keep his/her end of the bargain. Your best friend let you down. It's been a tough year financially. That bunch up there at the church did (or didn't)....! Life has dealt you a low blow. Your kids are all turning out bad. I know, you are not giving anything else to the church because that tele-evangelist did (or didn't)??.....! Yeah, you have had a bad headache all day. Your marriage is on the rocks. Your parents mistreated (or abused) you as a child. You could have played football if, so-in-so had (or hadn't) done......!

I know, you have been stricken with a chronic case of the "Monday Morning Mully Grubs." For God's sake, quarantine yourself! That stuff is contagious. The disease you are spreading is a serious stomach disorder, called 'Belly Aching.' Be sure to call a doctor immediately. Don't allow it to spread any further! It has already reached epidemic proportions in the secular world and many specialists believe it will come to that in the church. Those infected with this disease need a check-up, from the neck up, plus a heart transplant.

In the church, those that have contacted this infection are carriers, and need to be quarantined immediately. Those that truly love the Lord are concerned about it spreading all across the church and are praying for God to send a healing revival. It has actually reached a flood stage in some quarters of the Body of Christ. The contagion has actually come to the place that a new movement has developed. It is called *"The Sect of the Complainant Christians."*

If you have any symptoms such as complaining, gripping, belly-aching, murmuring, blaming others, fretting, stewing, continuously fussing, crying and whining, get checked immediately! How long has it been since you had a physical? Or a spiritual? What about an attitude check? If you have gone so far as to join the *'Complainant Movement,'* check yourself in at the Emergency Room of the nearest hospital. There are Infectious Disease Specialists that can diagnose your case and get treatment started immediately. They will, no doubt, put you in the Critical Care Unit and watch you 24 hours a day.

Why CCU? Because the disease can be fatal! These diagnostic specialists know exactly what they are looking for. They will run you through a battery of tests, define the symptoms and pronounce you to be a chronic complainer.

Actually, Dr. Jeremiah, peering through the telescope of time, made this diagnosis of your case:

> *"Why do you cry out because of your hurt [the natural result of your sin]? Your pain is deadly (incurable). Because of the greatness of your perversity and guilt, because your sins are glaring and innumerable, I have done these things to you."* (Jeremiah. 30:15, Amp.)

The specialists will not have to resort to their medical journals, they can know by your chronic complaining what your problem is. They will not have to be around you long before they notice that you *dislike everything* they and others do. It will be evident that you say you are innocent of all the charges brought against you. The tenor or spirit of your speech will be loaded with *blame for others*, and not yourself. You will *continuously make yourself look like a martyr.* They will notice as they converse with you that everybody has always mistreated you. These specialists will immediately become aware of a *continuous flow of excuses* for your failures and irresponsibilities.

> *"Be hospitable to one another without complaint."* (I Peter 4:9, NASB)

Have you caught on yet? You are sick! You need help! Are you not aware of the halitosis of your attitude? In the Bible, the word "spirit," is wind or breath. You have a serious attitude problem.

Let me ask you a few questions. What's wrong with everyone else? If you are always right, how does that leave others? Why do you blame everyone them? Why is it their fault? You were in it just as deep as they were, why are they to blame? Are you not aware that you possess what is called a 'martyr complex'? Why all the excuses?

Wake up! 'Fess up! Your days of fooling people have passed. Those that have to put up with your negative, complaining attitude, saw you for what you are a long time ago.

One of my best friends told me about sitting in a pastor's study, pouring out his heart to the concerned pastor who listened with interest and compassion. My friend, whom I will call Seigfried, was reared in a dysfunctional family whose father was extremely overbearing. Seigfried had many scars. Many memories. Bitterness and unforgiveness. It took several visits for him to receive the healing he so desperately needed.

On one visit the pastor helped him walk back through his battered childhood. They recalled each experience that had left many scars, heartaches and unpleasant memories, in its wake. The pastor asked Seigfried to go home and reflect on the memories that haunted him. He instructed him to make a list of all those individuals that had abused him, sharing what it was and how he felt in his heart about each situation. He did exactly as instructed.

My friend, in sincere repentance, gave these things back to God. He gave up the bitterness. He spoke 'forgiveness' to his father and all who had abused him in any way. Now, Praise God! Seigfried, has repented of his hard feelings, the bitterness, and has released all the hurt. He forgave every incident.

The pastor, knowing that my friend had received a heart void of offense, picked up the papers listing all his hurts, heartaches and bitterness. He held them in his hand for a few moments, then tore them into shreds. Looking very intently at Seigfried, he said, "From now on, it's your own fault!"

Some day you will have to come to the realization that the responsibility will be turned over to you. You will not be able to shirk it forever, by blaming everyone else. You will come to the end of your own dead-end street. You will have one alternative. You can make an about-face, turn 180 degrees and go back in the direction you came. This direction is right opposite from the way you have been going. Do it the right way for a change.

The attitude and action of your way of life is indeed sin, and it breaks harmony, wherever you are, as you unload your poison on those around you.

The Bible speaks directly to you and your situation. Notice what the Apostle says about it.

"Do all things without grumbling and faultfinding and complaining [against God] and questioning and doubting [among yourselves]." (Philippians 2:14, Amp.)

The Apostle also reflected on Israel, and their grumbling attitude, as they wandered about in the wilderness. He brought this to the attention of the Corinthians because they had a similar attitude problem about the Apostle himself (I Corinthians 10:9 & 10). Let's look at the references to the original account of Israel in the wilderness (Amp.).

"We should not tempt the Lord [try His patience, become a trial to Him, critically appraise Him, and exploit His goodness] as some of them did-and were killed by poisonous serpents; (Numbers 21:5 & 6) nor discontentedly complain as some of them did-and were put out of the way entirely by the destroyer (death). (Numbers 16: 41 & 49)

It makes good sense to me that every individual who has this type of complaining and grumbling spirit should make every attempt to get healed immediately. Let me offer this word of hope offered by the Prophet Isaiah.

"Those who err in spirit will come to understanding, and those who murmur [discontentedly] will accept instruction."

(Isaiah 29:24, Amp.)

Pray the above scripture for your self and ask God to give you a teachable spirit. Believe Him, that He will open your heart to accept and receive His instruction. He said it was possible, so receive it for yourself.

72

Chapter 20

You Do Not

Have To Compromise Your Integrity

That's right. You can give of your best to God and not to Satan. The writer of Hebrews posed a very pertinent question that I desire to address at this point. He asked, *"How shall we escape if we neglect so great salvation?"* (Heb. 2:3). The key word in his question is *"Neglect."* This word comes from the Greek word, *"ameleo,"* which means *"to be careless, not to care"* (*'a,'* means 'negative' & *'melo'* means to care or to be a care). So, the word means *"to be careless" or "make light of."*[21]

Negligence

If you are a Christian, you should display a life of holiness and good Christian integrity. You should not allow Satan to tempt you into compromising that integrity. But, it can be done easily by carelessness. If you do not appreciate the cleansing blood of Jesus, you can forget its importance and forfeit it by negligence. And what you are actually doing is *"making light of"* your salvation. If you make light of your salvation, someday you will come to the place where *"there is no escape."* This is especially true when you know that God has built into the fabric of your salvation certain preventive measures to eliminate such a disaster. Let's look at a couple of them in the First Epistle of John.

"… These things write we unto you, that your joy may be full. This then is the message which we have heard of Him, and declare unto you, that God is light, and in Him is no darkness at all. If we say we have fellowship with Him, and walk in darkness, we lie, and do not the truth: But if we walk in the light, as He is in the light, we have fellowship one with another, and the blood of Jesus Christ His Son, cleanseth us from all sin. If we say we have no sin, we deceive ourselves, and the truth is not in us. If we confess our sins, He is faithful and just to forgive us our sins, and to cleanse us from all unrighteousness." (1 John 1:4 - 9)

Be sure to notice in the above printed scripture, that God has made available some safeguards to keep us from compromising the integrity we have in Him. *God is light, and in Him there exists no darkness at all.* If we walk in that light the barriers that would prevent Christian fellowship are removed. **This eliminates discord among the brethren.** *Then the blood of Jesus flows again, and cleanses from all sin. This is 'present-tense' cleansing.*

Another measure God has made available to us, to keep us from yielding to temptation and compromising with Satan, is the confession of sin. We are not saying there is no sin, (see I John 1:10) we are simply saying that we do not have to allow it to be our destruction. *Confession of sin in the life of the believer brings two things to our rescue, forgiveness and total cleansing.*

A person can compromise his God-given cleansing by negotiating at the bar of temptation. I will be quick to say, *"No Christian should, by any means or under any circumstances, negotiate with Satan."* There is not enough common ground to even attempt to make negotiation feasible.

When we advise you not to surrender your integrity, we are simply stating the fact that you do not have to commit sin. Yes, you read it correctly, *'You do not have to sin.'*

Who told you that you could sin? Don't you know it is illegal! *Who* gave you the permission to sin, anyway? *Where* did you read or hear, that "you cannot help it, you have to sin everyday?" You did not receive your permission to sin from the Word of God, where it is prohibited. God hates sin.

Sin and Sins

Before we proceed further I need to explain what I am leading us into. Next, we will explore several definitions of 'sin' and attempt to blend a theological approach with a practical conclusion, as to what sin actually is. But right now I want to look at two aspects of sin and how they relate to the Christian life and living.

Innate And Overt Sin (Sin and Sins)

First, there is *sin as a principle.* Sin as a principle is a ***condition of the human heart.*** This ***innate sin*** is what some theologians call *'inbred sin.'* We are born with it. It is there to plague us and entice us to yield to temptation. Again, it is a *condition, a state of being, or an inward inclination to commit sin.* **Innate sin** is what causes the other aspect of sin. Because of **innate sin**, I have the nature of a sinner. Innate sin is inside the human heart and can be camouflaged or covered up, temporarily.

The other aspect of sin is *'that which is committed,' an overt act.* **Overt sin** is that which exposes innate sin. Another way to express it is, that overt sin is a symptomatic expression of the basic condition (innate sin). Overt sin is not hidden. It is sin that you commit. People commit sin (overt) because their hearts are sinful (innate). So really, what we are saying is that sin can be in two places: in the heart and in the hand. *One is what you are and the other is what you do. It is the being of sin that prompts and promotes the doing of sin.*

Jeremiah, the Prophet, said of the human heart, it *"Is deceitful above all things, and desperately wicked"* (Jeremiah 17:9). He is simply diagnosing the case of the human heart. His diagnosis is that the heart of man is *'sin-central'* of the individual, and from it overt sin is issued. Sin (innate), as a principle, is what entices or prompts man to commit sin (overt).

If you desire a second opinion on your case, Jesus offers one, but it is a confirmation of Jeremiah's original diagnosis. Jesus not only verified the exactness of the prophet's prediction, but also gave a list of evils that surface from the human heart because of its corrupt nature. Let's explore the Lord's analysis of the heart and learn how He explained it.

> *"That which proceeds out of the man, that is what defiles the man. For from within, out of the heart of men, proceed the evil thoughts, fornications, thefts, murders, adulteries, deeds of coveting and wickedness, as well as deceit, sensuality, envy, slander, pride and foolishness. All these evil things proceed from within and defile the man"* (Mark 7:20 - 23, NASB).

In this passage our Lord is depicting both the *innate* and the *overt* sin. He goes immediately to the source and then moves to the diabolical possibilities of what an evil heart can produce. It is not that which goes into the man that defiles him. It is that which comes out, because *that* is what is inside. Your outer life is your reputation with man and your inner life is your reputation with God. From God's vantage point both parts of our being is open to Him.

In Romans 3:23, Paul said, *"All have sinned and come short of the glory of God."* In this passage he was talking about sins committed and guilt incurred. Later on in Romans 7 he said, *"I am carnal, sold under sin"* (v.14), and spoke about *"Sin that dwelleth in me"* (v.17 & 20), he is not relating to sins committed, but expressing an awareness of an inner condition he could easily recognize. Sin is not simply an overt act, but any attitude or emotion which is less than Christ-like.

Overt Sin

Now, let's take a look at the overt sin that is committed because of the innate sin or the sin-principle within. What is sin? Exactly what are we dealing with when we talk about sinning? I shall go into more detail later, but at this juncture, let me just use one word or expression to make it simpler. The word that will get us started is *'disobedience'* or *'transgression'*. Sin is *disobedience to God and/or His law* (see I John 3:4). The other definitions that we shall explore are theological and practical ways of explaining man's disobedience to God.

What Is Sin?

Across the years, as I have studied sin and it's ill effects I have dealt with it in my own heart, as well as attempted to teach others how to avoid it. I have gleaned the definitions and meanings listed below from years of study as I have wrestled with this very unpopular topic, both in my life and in my teaching. Most of the references and some of the definitions move in and out of my memory and faded notes like an object moving in and out of the fog. So please accept these references, etc., as my most honest opinion for each source.

I suppose the most popular and generally used definition of sin is that it is: *"Missing the mark."* This is so general that it would be difficult to give credit to any one individual. We will touch on it later and find its source in the Bible.

"Sin is a God defying disposition," the late Dr. Paul S. Rees.

"Sin is deviation from the holiness of God," Dr. William B. Coker, Professor at Asbury College, Wilmore, Kentucky.

"Sin is the will of the creature pitted against the will of the Creator," H. L. Roush, Belpre, Ohio.

"Sin is going your own way, planning your own life according to your own will, without seeking the will of God," Porter Barrington, The Christian Life New Testament.[22]

Another expression or definition of sin is that it is *"An act of treason against the Kingdom of God."* (sorry, my notes and my memory have failed me as to the source of this one).

Adam committed high treason in The Garden of Eden and sold us all into sin. Mankind remained true to this part of his heritage and has continued to be a traitor to God's Kingdom. It seems as though sinning just comes naturally, but if we have been regenerated by the Blood of Jesus and the supernatural work of the Holy Spirit, it should not come naturally. The dynamic and dramatic experience of the new birth has put us in a different position. We have been *'born-all-over-again'* by the Spirit of the Resurrected Jesus, and His resurrected life is alive in us. We are indeed transformed by this spiritual and sacred transaction. Any violation of that transformation is treason. The Spirit of the Living God lives in the regenerated spirit of the born-again child of God. Sin will defile His Holy dwelling place or temple.

The previously listed definitions of 'sin' have come to us from the prolific pens of Godly scholars of the Bible. I am indebted to them for helping me get a more practical grip on some of the aspects of sin. They helped me to see more of what I am, the extreme importance of God's amazing grace, the blood of Jesus and the redemption of the Cross of Jesus Christ.

We are not through giving definitions of this thing called 'sin,' but let us, at this point, move directly into the Word of God for more direct shots at 'sin.' Listed below are scripture verses that shoot like an arrow to the point of our study, and simply say, "This is sin."

SIN IS TRANSGRESSION OF THE LAW. *"Whosoever committeth sin transgresseth also the law: for sin is the transgression of the law"* (I John 3: 4). Transgression is to step over the line, go aside, or go beyond that which is allowed by God.

SIN IS LAWLESSNESS OR REBELLION. *"…The law is not made for a righteous man, but for the lawless and disobedient, for the ungodly and for sinners, for unholy and profane…"* (I Timothy

1:9). Lawlessness is insurrection, revolution, disorder, bedlam, chaos, etc.

UNBELIEF IS SIN. When the Comforter *"is come, He will reprove the world of sin, and of righteousness, and of judgment: of sin because they believe not on me..."* (John 16: 8 & 9). Failing to believe is an indictment on the truth of God. It insults His Divinity, His Word, His Holiness, yea, His everything.

Notice also what John, the beloved, said in his first epistle: *"He that believeth on the Son of God hath the witness in himself: he that believeth not on God hath made him a liar; because he believeth not the record that God gave of His Son"* (I John 5:10).

TO TRESPASS IS SIN. *"...You hath He quickened,* **who were dead in trespasses and sins;** *Wherein in time past ye walked according to the* **course of this world**, *according to* **the prince of the power of the air, the spirit that now worketh in the children of disobedience"** (Ephesians 2:1 & 2). To trespass is to push your own will into the realm of God's authority. It is a deviation from uprightness and truth.

ERROR IS SIN. "...The wrath of God is revealed from heaven against all ungodliness and unrighteousness of men, who hold the truth in unrighteousness" (Romans 1:18). The person is deceived, especially if he thinks he is right.

ANY OR ALL UNRIGHTEOUSNESS IS SIN. (1 John 5:17). Unrighteousness is any move away from that which the Bible teaches to be righteous.

ALL INIQUITY IS SIN. In addressing the common guilt of mankind, the Apostle Paul wrote, *"When they knew God, they glorified Him not as God, neither were they thankful; but became vain in their imaginations, and their foolish heart was darkened. Professing themselves to be wise, they became fools, and changed the glory of the incorruptible God into an image made like to corruptible man, and to birds and four-footed beasts, and creeping things"* (Romans 1: 21 - 23).

After his gross sin with Bathsheba, and all the trimmings that accompanied this immorality, David cried out to God in utter desperation, and said, *"Hide Thy face from my sins, and blot out all mine iniquities"* (Psalm 51:9). Iniquity is an inherent and gross evil whether expressly forbidden or not.

Metaphorically speaking, **SIN IS MISSING THE MARK**. This was alluded to earlier but without much detail. Let's look at it again. One word used for 'sin' is the Hebrew word, 'chata,' which means, *"to miss, be guilty, forfeit purity."* Another use is the "sense of missing the mark or the path." A prime example of the use of the word 'chata' is in Judges 20:16. It says that there were 700 left-handed warriors in the Tribe of Benjamin who *"Could sling stones at a hair breadth, and not miss."*[23] Do you think it is ironic that 700, the number of completion or perfection, would never miss?

When Paul said, *"All have sinned and come short of the glory of God"* (Romans 3:23), he was showing us *how much* we missed the mark. Because of Adam's transgression, all mankind fell far below the exalted and manifested perfection of God. *We missed it!* It is, as it were, *our aim was too low.*

But, Praise God, we can raise our sights. The Apostle Paul, who said "We have fallen too short of God's perfection and glory," also said *"I press toward the mark"* (Philippians 3:14)! The word **'press,'** in the original language means **"to pursue or to press on."** Paul had his eye on the **'mark,'** *"the mark of the prize of the high calling of God in Christ Jesus"* (Philippians 3:14). We can aim toward perfection. In verse 12 Paul said, It is *"Not as though I had already attained, either were already perfect: but I follow after, if that I may apprehend that for which also I am apprehended of Christ Jesus."*

Even though we have indeed missed the mark, we have something we can set our eyes upon (Psalm 121:1 & 2). It is the mark of the prize of the high calling of God in Christ. None of us are perfect, and none have arrived or attained, but we can press on. It is amazing that the same word (in the Greek) that Paul used for 'press' in verse 14, is the same word used for 'follow' back in verse 12. It also means, *'to pursue without hostility.'* Yes, we can pursue Him and we can do it in the same direction we have fallen so short of. *I can easily say, "We can pursue perfection without hostility."* Without hostility on our part, because we are moving in the same direction as God. When a Christian is sinning, he is counter-productive to the things God is attempting to do.

79

So, my friend, let's go on our way *"forgetting those things which are behind, reaching forth to those things which are before"* (v.13). **LET'S GO ON TO PERFECTION** (Heb. 6:1)!

Sin is anything that sabotages the relationship between God and regenerate man. Sin contaminates the holiness of God in man. One of the previously stated quotes stated that, *"Sin is deviation from the holiness of God."* To me this is the simplest definition I have run across in my 43 plus years of study.

You Do Not Have To Commit Sin

In this last chapter we are dealing with the fact that we do not have to compromise our integrity. Sin, in whatever definition we work from, is the little fox that destroys the vines of integrity and any other kind of spiritual fruitfulness and progress. In all that we have discussed throughout this book it is sin that is at the root of it all. It is sin, in whatever guise it may take, that causes Christians to compromise their integrity. So, let's deviate from, *'You Do not Have To Compromise Your Integrity,'* and restate it: *"You Do Not Have to Commit Sin."* Let's ask some questions to stimulate our thinking: "How do I know that I do not have to commit sin? What is the basis of this kind of thinking? Where did this kind of philosophy originate? Do we have any Bible for such a 'way-out' doctrine?"

'The Privilege of not Committing Sin',

Has Not Been Taught Sufficiently

We stated earlier that we do not have to commit sin and we need to follow through on that. The reason for my entire premise on this fact is that **IT HAS NOT BEEN TAUGHT**. Very few evangelicals, unless they are of the Wesleyan or holiness persuasions, have spoken out on the matter. And because of this silence many Christians do not know that they have an option. Therefore, the questions of 'Is it wrong?' or 'Do I have to?' or 'What does the Bible say about it?' very seldom surfaces. They don't even think it is necessary. Some people just seem to take the attitude of: *'No news is good news;'* or *'Out of sight, out of mind;'* or *'If it ain't broke, don't fix it;'* or *'Ignore it, it'll go away;'* or *'Let sleeping dogs lie!'*

In this case 'no news is bad news.' It's time for somebody to break the silence and tell people they do not have to get caught up in this vicious cycle of disobedience to God and obeisance to the devil.

It does not have to happen! God grant that many dedicated Christians would wake up, sound the alarm, announce the deliverance and set the captive free. They definitely need to know that *the shackles have been broken and that Calvary is real.*

If it is 'out of sight,' again, it is because nobody's taking a stand to tell Christians 'you do not have to be the devil's whipping boy!' The Bible tells any interested reader that sin is deceitful (Heb. 3:13). If we would obey the admonition of this scriptural context it would not be 'out of sight,' nor 'out of mind.' Ponder it.

> *"[...Beware] brethren, take care, lest there be in anyone of you* **a wicked, unbelieving heart [which refuses to cleave to, trust in, rely on Him], leading you to turn away and desert or stand aloof from the living God. But instead warn (admonish, urge, and encourage) one another everyday, as long as it is called Today,** *that none of you may be hardened [into settled rebellion]* **by the deceitfulness of sin [by the fraudulence, the stratagem, the trickery which the delusive glamour of his sin may play on him].** (Heb. 3:12, 13, Amp.)

First, we are given a warning that this kind of attitude and behavior can creep in. **Secondly,** the mentality that thinks that a little sin, now and then, is alright can easily lead people to turn away from God. **Thirdly,** we are admonished to warn others everyday. **Fourthly,** we warn them because their hearts can become hardened to the point of rebellion. **Fifthly,** we can become so deceived that we are actually ignorant to the **fact of sin** and to the **terrible tragedy that it ultimately leads to**. This is where many are living today and they know not that the Bible has a resolution for this perplexing predicament.

Then, others might be saying, *it ain't broke, don't fix it!'* **I beg your most humble pardon, IT IS BROKE!** It is indeed in a sad state of repair. And, it definitely needs fixing. It is broken because so very few are teaching people that they do not have to yield to the temptation presented to them by the forces of evil. Temptation is not sin, but it is solicitation to do evil sponsored by Satan. Christians need to know that they do not have to play the devil's silly game. You say, "Well, I never thought of it!" There is a good reason that you have never thought of it. It's because you probably never heard it. It is so badly broken that we have to write a book to draw people's attention

81

to it. It's radical! It's new! It's revolutionary! But, it is not new or radical, it is scriptural. Really and truly, it is indeed 'the way in.' *It's the only way in!*

Are you the one who is saying, *"Ignore it, it will go away?"* Many, many people are doing just that, ignoring it. That's the problem, *it has been ignored, and as a result, it has unleashed its devastating effects wherever it has been overlooked.* Wherever it has been allowed to breed and blend into the environment it has reached epidemic proportions. *It has not gone away! In thousands of years, it's still here.*

What about 'Letting sleeping dogs lie?' This is one sleeping dog we simply cannot allow to just lie there. We have tip-toed by him long enough. Why? Well, while he is lying there sin continues to rise above flood stage. Wake that sleeping dog and train him to be a watchdog! He will be most helpful if he can arouse us to receive at least three things in the Body of Christ. These three: We need to get Christian people to realize that *sin is a nuisance*. We need to get them to recognize sin's devastating consequences. We need to get them to understand the fact that they are not bound to it, *they are not bond slaves of Satan.* If we can get these needs supplied, then this barking dog will be that beeper that will sound the alarm in our consciences and alert us to the sin that is lurking in the shadows and prancing in the noon-day sun.

What We Are Saying and what We Are Not Saying

Let me tell you what we are saying and what we are not saying. We **ARE** saying, "You **DO NOT** have to commit sin!" We are **NOT** saying you **CANNOT** commit sin!" You **CAN** commit sin any time you desire and most of us get around to it sooner or later. Be sure to get this, God, nowhere, at anytime, has commanded us to sin.

Don't forget, you can sin anytime you choose, but you do not have to. Now, be sure to get a good tight grip on this fact: *"Sin is a choice. You sinned because you chose to. It is a decision that you make, it's an act of your own volition."* So, don't blame it on anyone else. Don't blame it on the circumstances. You made a choice, it was an act of your own will to commit that act of un-godliness.

I Don't Want To Do Evil

How happy I am when someone stands up and says that I have an option, that I have the privilege of not sinning! It is so refreshing because ***I do not want to sin against God or anyone else.*** I feel like you are the same way and you do not want to sin. Let me tell you why I do not want to sin.

It is illegal. It is a transgression of God's law, of His Holy commandments.

It is un-holy. It is an insult to the Holiness of God. When a born-again child of God commits sin, he disgraces God's Holy Image and profanes the Name of Jesus Christ. Notice what Israel, God's chosen people, did among the heathen. God was quick to alert them, through the Prophet Ezekiel, about their sin and un-holy conduct. God was especially provoked about the profane image His own people were projecting about Himself.

God said,

"…'I will vindicate the holiness of My great Name which has been profaned among the nations, which you have profaned in their midst. Then the nations will know that I am the Lord,' declares the Lord God, 'when I prove Myself holy among you in their sight'." (Ezekiel 36:23, NASB)

It weakens my witness for Christ. Some years ago a well known evangelist went out visiting, doing door-to-door evangelism. In order to train another person to do personal witnessing, he enlisted the help of another individual in the church. They had made their first contact and were ready to lead the candidate in the 'sinner's-prayer.' Everything was right. The stage was set. Just as they started to pray, the other individual pulled from his pocket a pack of cigarettes, removed one, and proceeded to light it. The convicted candidate for salvation lost her conviction and said to the evangelists, "If that is all you two have to offer, you may leave my house now, I am not ready for your kind of religion."

Let me leave this with you before we proceed further, ***Sin will drain your spiritual battery.*** There will be neither force nor fire in your ministry for Jesus, if you allow sin to reign and remain in your mortal body (Romans 6:12).

Sin distorts the Christian message. "Sinning Christians" cause lost people to fail to see the forest because of all the trees. They are preaching one thing and doing another. Don't you know that lost people can see that? Is there a slight chance that we might think we can con them? Maybe, but not often. The Christian message is good news and tells the truth of God's message of salvation and the fact that He saves us *FROM* sin and its penalties.

Sin has a deadening influence on the saved and the lost. It weakens the Christian and pushes the lost person further back into his unregenerate condition. It makes a Christian spiritually impotent in the face of temptation. That's the reason the Holy Spirit *convicts people of their sins.* It is next to impossible for 'sinning Christians' to advance the Kingdom of God. They have so little to offer that might lead a lost person to a saving knowledge of the truth. It is not worth our time to send them out.

Sinning dulls the Christian's conscience as to the cannibalistic effects of its nature. The more he indulges into this vicious Satanic conduct the more his mind becomes unaware of some of the schemes and devices of the devil. It keeps the individual from seeing many of the tragedies and ill effects of sin. Actually, he loses consciousness of what sin is all about. Therefore, he moves on into it without compunction of conscience.

It handcuffs the Christian when he is arrested by Satan through temptation. *Temptation is solicitation to do evil.* Notice what happens when a Christian yields to temptation:

> *"…Every man is tempted, when he is drawn away of his own lust and enticed. Then, when lust hath conceived, it bringeth forth sin: and sin, when it is finished, bringeth forth death."*
> (James 1:14 & 15)

Satan has some type of hypnosis he works on an individual to draw that person into his trap. That individual is drawn to Satan by that person's own individual lust. Sin and temptation are all around us. As long as we are in this world we can expect them to attempt to influence us. But, you know, we do not have to partake of any of it. What happens is this: We walk amid all the sin and temptation and are continually propositioned by them. We can eat of it's fruit or refuse it. But, something inside us is attracted to that outside influence, we are drawn away by our own lust and enticed. **If** we yield, we are enticed.

It goes from **temptation** to **lust** to **sin** and on to **death**. Remember, our environment is full of temptation. It is all around us all the time.

I repeat, temptation is all around us all the time. We can continually walk through it, but we are not tempted *until* we are *drawn away of our own lust and enticed.* The Amplified Version states it this way: *"...Every person is tempted when he is drawn away, enticed and baited by his own evil desire (lust and passions)."* You cause your own temptation. You cannot truthfully say, "The devil made me do it."

Sin weakens the Christian to the point of no resistance each time he yields to the temptation to any solicitation from Satan. As long as he continues to sin, his immune system becomes more and more deficient. He can contract **AIDS.**

'A. I. D. S.' is an acronym for *"Acquired Immune Deficiency Syndrome."* Be sure to note-it is acquired! Something in the life of that individual was acquired by something he was persistently involved in. What about another acronym? *Any Iniquity Destroys Strength (AIDS)!*

The more an individual delves into sin the weaker he becomes in times of temptation. His immune system heads down hill to a point of no return. *DON'T CHECK IT OUT!*

When I sin I give Satan inroads into my life. Satan is searching for ways to get into your life, whether in spirit, soul, or body. He stands ready to seize upon every opportunity we afford him. When we leave one small crack in our armor he takes advantage of it. When he goes in through that small crack, he makes it larger. From that he goes on to slip through every crack and crevice we leave for him. He is a sharp-shooter and can hit the target we leave open for him. But, with the shield of faith, we can extinguish all the fiery missiles of Satan (Ephesians 6:16). God does not expect us to leave any opening in our lives through sin.

The delusion and deceitfulness of sin causes hardness of heart (Heb. 3:13). Any individual Christian can be deluded and deceived by sin to the point of receiving a calloused and insensitive heart. When a person becomes hard in his heart, he is no longer able to truthfully say 'no' to sin. It does not burden his conscience to disobey God.

85

Sinning Is a Decision

God made man in His own Image and made him a free moral agent. Man has a choice. He has a prerogative. He can decide whether he will sin or not. He can make up his own mind whether he will obey or disobey. **TO SIN OR NOT TO SIN, THAT IS THE QUESTION! IT IS A CHOICE! IT IS YOUR DECISION!** It is not something you blame on someone else, or on the weather, or on the devil, or on the circumstances, or on your condition or on God. No, you cannot even blame it on Satan. The buck stops with you.

So it is with obedience. It's your decision. Moses **CHOSE** to suffer and endure ill treatment and affliction with the people of God, rather than enjoy the passing pleasures of sin as the son of Pharaoh' daughter (Heb. 11:25 & 26).

In reporting on the wilderness wanderings of the Israelites, the writer of Hebrews had this to say about their situation at a certain juncture in their travels. The Israelites **COULD NOT** enter into the Promised Land because of their unbelief. Two things kept Israel out of the Promised Land at that time: (1) Hardness of heart, and (2) Unbelief. The Bible teaches us that unbelief or failing to trust God, is sin (Romans 14:23). The Greek word from which *"could not"* was translated comes through in the NIV and the TEV as, *"Were not able."* Why? Why were they not able to enter in? Because they had sinned away their strength and ability to resist the onslaughts of Satan.

You Do Not Have To Sin!

Again, let me say, because of your sinful nature and your God-given prerogative to choose, *you can sin anytime you desire.* Another thing I need to say at this point is that most of us go ahead and sin anyway, regardless of what God or the devil might have to say about it. Solomon said, *"..There is not a just man upon earth, that doeth good, and sinneth not"*(Ecclesiastes 7:20), meaning that all of us have the capacity to do so. But again, we do not *HAVE to do so.*

Satan is for it and God is against it. So, the ball is in our court and we can go with God or go with Satan. Satan is always trying to get people to yield to his temptation. The other side of that coin is the fact that God, nowhere tempts people to commit sin. In fact, Jesus, in the Model Prayer, or the Lord's Prayer, prayed to the Heavenly Father,

"Lead us not into temptation, but deliver us from evil." We learned earlier that sin is disobedience to God. There is no place in the Bible where God says that we have to sin or disobey Him. In fact, the reverse of that is the only way we should go.

Indulge with me a few more minutes and let's learn how the Bible assesses sin. In so doing let the Word of God assure us that the pressure that comes upon us as temptation is not from God.

The Apostle Paul has much to say about this subject. So much, that I cannot deal with all of it, so permit me to look at a portion that starts off with Christ's death and the finished work of Calvary.

"…By the death He died, He died to sin [ending His relation to it] once for all; and the life that He lives, He is living to God [in unbroken fellowship with Him]. *Even so* **consider yourselves also dead to sin and your relation to it broken,** but alive to God [living in unbroken fellowship to Him] in Christ Jesus. **Let not sin therefore rule as king in your mortal (short lived, perishable) bodies,** to make you yield to its cravings and be subject to its lusts and evil passions. **Do not continue offering your bodily members [and faculties] to sin as instruments (tools) of wickedness. But offer and yield yourselves to God as though you have been raised from the dead to [perpetual] life, and your bodily members [and faculties] to God,** presenting them as instruments of righteousness. **For sin shall not [any longer] exert dominion over you, since now you are not under the Law [as slaves], but under grace** [as subjects of God's favor and mercy]. What then [are we to conclude]? *Shall we sin because we are not under the Law but under God's favor and mercy? CERTAINLY NOT!"* (Romans 6:10 - 15 Amp.)

This passage sheds light on this entire study of things we 'do not have to do,' as well as this last one on 'not having to commit sin.' This entire passage puts the ball in our court by telling us *"In the same way"* (NIV & Phillips), that Jesus died to sin and ended His relationship with it, we too must do the same. And consider ourselves as dead to the appeal and power of sin.

I think it worthy to note that the above cited scripture begins with Christ's death and atonement on the cross. And we could say, "that's where it starts." Yes, that's where salvation began. But, it is also where it stops! It is indeed the place where sin can stop! The writer of Hebrews stated, *"…Jesus…, That He might sanctify the people with*

His own blood, suffered without (outside) the gate" (Hebrews 13:12). The blood shed by Jesus on the cross was for the purpose of taking away sin. The sacred writer was alluding to the scapegoat on which the sins of Israel were laid. The goat was sacrificed 'outside the gate' of the camp during their wilderness wanderings. That's where Jesus was sacrificed, outside the gate of the city of Jerusalem. The sin question was settled at Calvary. I know that we still have to contend with it, but let's do all in our power to leave sin under the blood. Jesus died to forgive all your sins (Colossians 2:13 & I John l: 7 & 9).

We Do Not Have To Commit Sin, But In Order To Be Able 'Not To', There Are Some Things That We Must Do.

Let's look at some things we are admonished to do that shows we have a choice in the matter and that we do NOT have to be a part of all the sin that rages around us. From the scripture cited above (Romans 6:10 - 15, Amp.). **(1) We need to consider our relation to sin broken. (2) We should not allow sin to reign(rule) in our frail human bodies. (3) We should not continually yield our bodily members and faculties to sin because they will be used as tools of wickedness.** If this happens there is nothing we can say because we yielded to the devil. **(4) The flip side of that is the fact that we can yield our members and faculties to God and they will become instruments and tools in God's hands for righteousness and holiness. (5) God lets us know very emphatically that sin does not have to rule over us because we are not under the Law, but under God's saving and delivering grace. (6) Then, Paul brings us to a practical conclusion. He puts it in the form of a question and then gives God's answer. "Shall we sin because we are not under the Law but under God's favor and mercy?"** His answer is very simple. *"CERTAINLY NOT!"* The KJV says, *"GOD FORBID."*

Many things have been stated already that show us why we should not commit sin, or states the fact that we do not want to sin. Let's continue to look at some reasons why sin is an unnecessary item on our agenda of activities, the little foxes that spoil the vines. I feel like you could say with me, **"I DO NOT WANT TO SIN BECAUSE:"**

Sin Is Forbidden!

In the previously cited context from Romans Chapter 6, we noticed that The apostle Paul asked us a very pertinent question:

"Shall we sin because we live not under the Law but under God's favor and mercy?" His answer to this very important question was blunt and to the point, *"Certainly not!"* As you remember, the KJV puts it even clearer, **"GOD FORBID!"** Don't panic, you'll see this phrase again.

The Apostle John records an account of a man who had been sick for thirty eight years. He had lain by the pool of Bethesda for an extremely long time. At certain seasons an angel of the Lord would come down and stir the waters. The first person to get into the waters, after they had been stirred, would be healed. Jesus knew the situation and asked the man if he desired to be healed. Jesus healed the man without the man being put in the water. Later that day Jesus saw him and said to him, *"DO NOT SIN ANYMORE, so that nothing worse may come on you "*(John 5:14).

The New Testament relates another story where Jesus spoke very frankly about this matter of sin. There was brought to Him a woman caught in the very act of adultery, she was still naked. She cowered before Him and her accusers. But Jesus, rather than add to her shame, bowed His head. During this time her accusers continued to make their accusations, hoping to pressure Jesus into doing something they could use to condemn Him. Sensing their deceit and hostilities, Jesus spoke to them and said, *"He who is without sin among you, let him be the first to throw a stone at her"* (John 8:7, NASB). While His head was still bowed, with His finger, He wrote something in the sand. No one knows exactly what He wrote. But, for some reason, the accusers left, rather hurriedly. When the Master raised His head there was no one to accuse the woman.

Jesus spoke directly to her and said, *"Woman, where are they? Did no one condemn you?* Her answer was, *"No one, Lord."* To which Jesus replied, *"Neither do I condemn you; go your way, FROM NOW ON SIN NO MORE"* (John 8:10 & 11, NASB, emphasis mine.). I don't know how it is in your spiritual economy, but **JESUS FORBIDS SIN.**

Paul, the Apostle, felt the same way Jesus did about the fact that sin is forbidden. He told the Church at Rome to consider themselves dead to sin (6:11), and therefore, they should not allow sin to reign or rule in their mortal bodies (v. 12). And further said to them *"Sin SHALL NOT be master over you"* (v. 14, NASB). Then he posed a question, asking them if they should continue to sin since they were not under the law, but under grace. His answer? **GOD FORBID!** This is the third time we have repeated this strong stand the Bible takes against sin. But it is our desire that every individual allow these two words, **"GOD FORBID!"** to vibrate and echo through the chambers of his soul, especially when he is confronted by an opportunity to commit sin.

In writing to the sin-latent people in Corinth, he shot straight to the heart and said, *"Become sober-minded as you ought, AND STOP SINNING..."* (I Corinthians 15:34, NASB)! The Apostle John was of the same school of thought because he listened to the same Holy Spirit. In his first epistle, John said, *"My little children, these things write I unto you, THAT YE SIN NOT. And if any man sin, we have an advocate with the Father, Jesus Christ, the righteous"* (I John 2:1, emphasis mine). Don't forget, Christian, God forbids sin. You can go ahead and sin, if you so desire, but you will pay an enormous price for it. Sin is so expensive no Christian can afford it.

Sin Is An Abomination To God

This means **God's hates sin, it is detestable to Him**. Notice below seven things God hates.

(1) A proud or haughty look.

(2) A lying tongue.

(3) Hands that shed innocent blood.

(4) A heart that devises wicked plans.

(5) Feet that run rapidly to evil.

(6) A false witness that speaks lies.

(7) An individual that spreads strife and discord among the brothers. (Proverbs 6:16 - 19)

Other things are mentioned, throughout the Bible, that God hates. But the bottom line of it all is that *God hates sin*. Any sin will operate like one of those little foxes and undermine everything you do.

Sinning Is Grounds For Divorce

Sanctification is separation **to** God. Sin is separation **from** God. Notice how the Prophet Isaiah accessed this thing of sin against God.

"Surely the arm of the Lord is not too short to save, nor His ear too dull to hear. But your iniquities have separated you from God; your sins have hidden His face from you, so that He will not hear." (Isaiah 59:1 & 2, NIV)

God wants you, and it is obvious, He does not want your sin. **But, if you love sin more than you love God, its time to file for divorce.** You will not have to initiate these divorce procedures, it will be taken care of for you, if you persist in sinning.

Sinning Carries The Death Penalty

That's right! If you continue on in your little (any sin is large in God's sight) game of sin, you are signing your own death warrant. *"As righteousness tendeth to life: so he that pursueth evil pursueth it to his own death"* (Proverbs 11:19). Look at some more little spot sermons that caution the Christian about his 'grave digging' activity, called sinning.

"The soul that sinneth, it shall die." (Ezek. 18:4)

"...By one man sin entered the world, and death by sin; and so death passed upon all men, for that all have sinned." (Romans 5:12)

"...The wages of sin is death; but the gift of God is eternal life through Jesus Christ our Lord." (Romans 6:23)

Sinning Bears Its Own Fruit

Just prior to Paul's listing of the Fruit of the Spirit, he gives some of the fruit of sin, which he calls 'the works of the flesh.'

"The works of the flesh are manifest, which are these; Adultery, fornication, uncleanness, lasciviousness, idolatry, witchcraft, hatred, variance, emulations, wrath, strife, seditions, heresies, envyings, murders, drunkenness, revellings, and such like: of which I tell you before, as I have also told you in times past, that they which do such things shall not inherit the Kingdom of God." (Galatians 5:19-21)

If you commit any of the sins listed above, they become the fruit of your life. It was in the soil of your life that they came forth. Any one of these sins portray a poor witness for and a poor image of the sinless Son of God, Jesus Christ. All of Satan's practices are attractive, seductive, infective, addictive, and finally, destructive.

Committing Sin Is Inexcusable

There is no excuse for sin. If you sin, you can move in one of two directions: (1) You can live with it and pay the price for it, or, (2) You can seek and receive God's forgiveness. But there is no excuse or justification. God does not sanction sin.

The Apostle Paul, in sharing the course sin had taken, and the obvious effect it had wrought on those who had surrendered to it, said God has given them over to their own *'vile affections and degrading passions.'* Man is still without excuse, because the Gospel had been preached. The Gospel is revelation about the righteousness of God, **AND** the wrath of God. Paul said:

"Ever since the creation of the world His (God's) invisible nature and attributes, that is, His eternal power and divinity, have been made intelligible and clearly discernible in and through the things that have been made (His handiworks). So [men] are without excuse [altogether without any defense or justification]." (Romans 1:20, Amp.)

The only hope for mankind is that they plead for salvation through Jesus and the finished work of Calvary.

Jesus, in talking about the Jews and the Pharisees in particular, told His disciples that the Jews hated them because they hated Jesus first. The Jews persecuted the disciples of Jesus because the Jews did not know or understand God, the Father. He continues to speak to His disciples about the Jews:

"If I had not come and spoken to them, they would not be guilty of sin [would be blameless] but now they have no excuse for their sin." (John 15:22, Amp.)

They were inexcusable because Jesus had come. If you have Jesus in your life, there is no excuse for your sin. Forgiveness, yes, but no excuse.

Sinning Will Put You In Bondage

You will be bound by something that belongs to you, your own sin. Notice what Solomon said about sin and its ill consequences.

"His own iniquities shall snare the wicked man, and he shall be held by the cords of his own sin." (Proverbs 5:22, Amp.)

If it is your sin why don't you **stop it, NOW?**

Jesus said, **"Truly, truly, I say to you, everyone who commits sin is the slave of sin"** (John 8:34, NASB). 'Nuff said!'

Luke told us that when the Apostle Paul was approached by Simon, the Magician, in an attempt to bribe the Apostle, The Holy Spirit gave Paul a discerning spirit about Simon. The Apostle told the Magician, **"...I see that you are full of bitterness, and captive to sin"** (Acts 8:23, NIV). The Amplified Version says Simon was **"..In a bond forged by iniquity [to fetter souls]."**

Again, the Apostle Paul, looking at his own carnal nature, said, **"...I see a different law in the members of my body, waging war against the law of my mind, and making me a prisoner of the law of sin which is in my members"** (Romans 7:23, NASB).

Beware, sin will incarcerate you if you don't let it alone.

Sin Provokes The Wrath Of God

We told you before, "God hates sin." And to make it much simpler, Sin makes God mad! After listing several sins that call down God's wrath, the Apostle gives us a warning. He rather sternly cautions us about listening to many preachers and teachers who water down the gospel about sin and its heinous and atrocious results. Notice his special consternation and concern about dealing with sin.

> **"Let no man deceive you with vain words: for because of these things cometh the wrath of God upon the children of disobedience. Be not ye partakers with them."** (Ephesians 5:6 & 7)

The wrath of God is incurred upon those who are disobedient and do the things stated earlier. Then comes another stern warning, 'Don't even be partners with those individuals.'

There is no doubt about it, I don't want to sin, you do not want to sin and God doesn't want either of us to sin. The Bible makes it very clear that sin just does not have a legitimate place in the life of a Christian. So, reconcile yourself to the fact that sin is available and readily accessible, and make up your mind, to the best of your knowledge and ability, to have as little to do with it as possible. Why? Because the closer you walk to any kind of sin, the more the little foxes will creep in to spoil your vines. Committing sin is definitely a compromise of your integrity.

Now, for a more positive note, and for a conclusion on this last chapter, **GOD WANTS US TO BE HOLY**. In fact, that's the reason He originally made us in His Image. Oswald Chambers, in his sequel to, *"My Utmost For His Highest,"* *"Still Higher,"* is very bold in his belief that Christians should live a holy life. He speaks prophetically, *"A born-again soul is condemned to holiness; he is not at liberty to do what he likes but only what God likes, 'a bond slave of Jesus '...."*[24] How do we know that it is God's desire for us to be holy? (1) He allowed His Son to die for it (Heb. 13:12). (2) It is God's will for you to be sanctified (made holy) (I Thessalonians 4:3). (3) God Himself calls us to holiness (I Thessalonians 4:7 and 5:23 - 24). (4) He commands that we be holy (Leviticus 11:44 & 45; and I Peter 1:16).

In the October, 1993 issue of *Decision Magazine*, a contributing author, K. F. W. Prior, submitted an article entitled, *"Sanctification? What's That?"* Prior is of the same school of thought as we are, believing that God wants us to be holy. He speaks rather sternly and says, *"Because God Himself is holy, He demands holiness from His creatures."*[25]

You do not have to sin. You do not want to sin. I do not want you to sin. God does not want you to sin. The odds are against the devil in this matter. Stand firm on God's Word and remember God is on your side. No doubt you are saying, "I'm convinced that I do not have to commit sin, but how can I keep from it?" We have dedicated Appendix I of this book to give you God's Word on resisting the devil. It will not be a cure-all for your victory over sin, but if you will obey its commands you will be in a better position to say no to it. It will be much easier than before.

Appendix I

How Shall I NOT Sin?

From the beginning of this book until now, I have been addressing you as a born-again Christian. I shall continue to do so to the end. But, in order for this study to be of any positive, progressive, and permanent value to you, *you must be born again, born from above, born of God, born of the Holy Spirit, born all-over-again* (John 3:5, 6 & 7). If you have not been regenerated by the Holy Spirit, for your eternal well being, please read, study, meditate, and obey the following suggestions.

Agree with yourself that *you are lost and incapable of saving yourself* (Romans 3:23).

Accept the fact that *Jesus Christ is your only hope,* and that He alone can save you (Acts 4:10 - 12).

Accept the fact that God **IS** (He exists), and that *He is a rewarder of them that diligently seek Him* (Heb. 11:6).

Confess (speak it aloud) with your own mouth, *"Jesus Christ is my Lord"* (Romans 10:9). **Say it again, LOUDER!**

Believe in your own heart that God raised Jesus from the dead (Romans 10:9 & 10). Believe it! Say it! *"God raised Jesus from the dead!"*

Ask Jesus to indwell you, take up residence in your heart (Rev. 3: 20), and forgive you of all your sin. *Thank Him for saving you and living in you.*

Then, live like a Christian, BE ONE! You are one, if you diligently and sincerely followed through on all the above listed suggestions.

What Shall I Do That Will Help Keep Me From Yielding To Temptation?

Whatever we suggest below demands an extra, special effort on your part, plus a strong belief that God's grace will continue to function on your behalf. Just starting is not enough, you must ***"Press toward the mark for the prize of the high calling of God in Christ Jesus"*** (Philippians 3:14). You will be marching from carnality to sanctity and the road is long, rugged, treacherous, and uphill all the way. This journey affords no place for pantywaists and conscientious objectors. So, if you are serious about your walk with God and your witness of His integrity, let's go for it! However, I admonish you to count the cost of taking such a bold step against the enemy.

Go With God

You must make a solid and quality decision and commitment to be in this for the long-haul. Set your sights on nothing short of the peak of this mountain. It might be encouraging to receive this vote of confidence, from the Apostle Paul, as you embark. ***"I am confident of this: that the One who has begun His good work in you will keep on developing it until the day of Jesus Christ"*** (Philippians 1:6, Phillips). *Be obedient to what you can do and **trust the Holy Spirit to do what you cannot do**.* It will demand great portions of grit, on your part, and grace on God's part, to pull this one off.

Marching Toward Sanctity

Our desire is to direct and instruct you in this *'walk of faith.'* This walk of faith is your *'growing-up'* in Christ Jesus. It can also be called your *'move toward Christian maturity,'* or, your, *'going-on-to-perfection'* (Heb. 6:1). But for this study, we will think of it as your growth toward sanctification. As you grow in grace you are growing up in holiness. The words, 'sanctification' and 'holiness' can be used correspondingly, because they mean essentially the same thing. Each of these English words originated in the same Greek word, *'hagiasmos,'* which "signifies *(a) separation to God* (I Corinthians 1:30; II Thessalonians. 2:13; I Peter 1:2). (b) The resultant state, *the conduct befitting those separated* (I Thess. 4:3, 4, & 7)."[26] I suppose the simplest way to express it is that *sanctification (or holiness) is the transfer from the profane to the sacred.*

What Is Holiness Not?

Holiness is not a 'holier than thou' or a sanctimonious attitude. Neither is it legalism. It is not a set of guidelines sent down from the denominational headquarters. Holiness or sanctification is not self-righteousness. It is not some preacher's idea of how long the ladies wear their dress lengths or cut their hair.

What Is Holiness?

Holiness is the character of Jesus Christ. It is the standard of living in heaven. Holiness is the standard of living in the church of the living Lord Jesus. It is the behavior befitting Christians. Holiness is a condition of the recreated human heart. I like to express it as *"purity and holiness of heart and Life."*

Three Phases of Holiness

It is very probable that you have been asking yourself, "Where is the Holy Spirit in all this?" Well, that's a very important question, because He (the Holy Spirit) is God's Special Agent in the entire process (Romans 15:16; I Corinthians 6:11; II Thessalonians 2:13; I Peter 1:2). Have you ever noticed that we, in protestant circles, very seldom call God, the Holy Father. Neither do we protestants very seldom call Jesus, the Holy Son. But, **we always call the Third Person of the Divine Trinity, the Holy Spirit.** Why? Because it is the mission and ministry of the Holy Spirit to make us holy!

He begins His royal purging at our new birth and carries it on through to heaven.

The First is the INITIAL PHASE. This Phase is in operation in your new birth experience. We call it The Birth of the Spirit (John 3:6). This is *Initial Sanctification.* The Holy Spirit begins his progressive work of purging and sanctifying you, on a very minute scale, at this particular juncture of your fellowship with Him.

The Next is the INTERMEDIATE PHASE. This phase is in operation in your experience of the fullness of the Holy Spirit. We call it The Baptism of the Spirit (Acts 1:5). It can also be called *Entire Sanctification.* When this Heavenly Guest takes full occupancy in your entire being (spirit, soul, & body, I Thess. 5:23), the temple is swept clean, wholly and completely. However, we are holding this treasure in earthen vessels (II Corinthians 4:7), and because of carnality, these old clay pots leak. Satan jumps in at this juncture and really moves upon us with all his schemes and devices. This calls for another phase of sanctification to kick in.

This one is the FINAL PHASE. This part or era of your earth walk is *Progressive Sanctification*. It is that 'growing-up' and advancing toward holiness. A well known premise of John Wesley is *"The Holy Spirit is the grace of God at work."* This, the Third Person of the Divine Trinity, administers the grace of God in all three of these phases of sanctification. He continues on from here perfecting the work He has already begun in you. He will do it until the day of Christ (Philippians 1:6). The Holy Spirit walks through the process with us, step by step. He is gently purging and helping us in every hurdle, especially as we allow Him to do so. Wow! What a companion we have to help us on our *upward expedition to holiness* of heart and life.

Triumphant March

Let's begin our study of this 'triumphant march' with a springboard from the Holy scriptures. In his second letter to the church at Corinth, the Apostle Paul flings a tremendous challenge to Christians.

> *"Since we have these promises, dear friends, let us purify ourselves from everything that contaminates body and spirit, perfecting holiness out of reverence for God."* (II Corinthians 7:1, NIV)

Paul had previously given them a command from out of the Old Testament. *"Come out from among them, be ye separate, and touch not the unclean"* (II Corinthians 6:17). This was a reference to promises made by God through the Prophet Ezekiel (20:34). It was simply a promise of deliverance, then and now. It holds true today, and, as it was then, carries a stipulation. The Bible is the contract which stipulates that we *"cleanse ourselves"* (KJV), in order to effect the perfecting of holiness in our lives.

Going On To Perfection

God desires that we go on to perfection (Heb. 6:1). Paul is suggesting that some would possibly say that this is a rare kind of perfection. He instructs us to make holiness perfect in our lives. According to Harrison, the phrase, "perfecting holiness, emphasizes the fact that the process is continuous."[27] Be sure to note that 'perfecting' is an on-going, present tense. This is a *'now'* experience, that continues on into the future.

Steps Toward Holiness

This triumphant march from our birth experience to our final approach to heaven, I will call 'Steps Toward Holiness.' We are marching! Marching to Zion! Webster says, to march is "To walk with regular, steady steps, as soldiers."

If you are interested in making this march, I challenge you to march "with regular, steady steps," like soldiers. I admonish you to know and remember that the Holy Spirit is your Drill Instructor. He will guide you all the way through the march. Be on the alert for His every command!

STEP 1. Make A Clean Break With Sin!

Paul told us earlier to *purify ourselves.* Up goes the red flags! "No, we cannot purify ourselves, Jesus is the only One Who can do that!" Before we can go any further, we must get over this hurdle and remove the thought that we cannot purify ourselves. *Firstly,* we know that God said, *"do it!"* What do you do with that? *Pray and obey!*

Secondly, Jesus has already done everything necessary for this to be accomplished. He has done His part already. It is indeed unnecessary for Him to repeat it. Now, the rest is left up to us. Jesus died in vain if we do not take the initiative and receive what He has already appropriated.

Then, *thirdly,* The previously cited scripture (II Corinthians 7:1) commands us to avail ourselves to the finished work of Calvary and allow His blood to flow through us, is not alone in admonishing us to do so.

Be sure to note, the Bible not only commands us to take the initiative and *'cleanse and purify ourselves,'* but we must do it *'out of reverence for God.'* The KJV says we do it *'In the fear of God.'* This is indeed a very serious admonition with devout reverence to His Holiness. Notice how Paul addressed this when directing Timothy on how to handle matters such as this, where people refuse to cleanse and purify themselves, and, as such, persist in sinning.

"...For those who are guilty and persist in sin, rebuke and admonish them in the presence of all, so that the rest may be warned and stand in wholesome awe and far." (I Timothy 5:20, Amp.)

Let's get serious, Friend, and shake ourselves into the sober reality, **God does not play games with sinners, sin or Satan!** Whatever happened to the fear of God in the church of the Living Lord Jesus? **"Be not deceived, God is not mocked: for whatsoever a man soweth, that shall he also reap".** (Galatians 6:7)

The Apostle John in his first epistle, shares the fact that we are the sons of God. The apostle admits that we do not know what we shall be like when Jesus comes. But he is sure of this, when Jesus does appear, **we shall be like Him.** Hallelujah! He continues by saying that every individual Christian should live in the hope of the soon return of Jesus. If we live in that hope, **we must purify ourselves as He is pure** (I John 3:1 - 3)! From the Amplified Version, although it is just as plain in the other versions, it says:

"... Everyone that has this hope [resting] on him cleanses (purifies) himself just as He is pure (chaste, undefiled, guiltless). "(I John 3:3)

It is something that God expects us to do. The ball is now in our court. We need to put up or shut up!

In His High Priestly prayer in John 17, the Lord offers us His own life application in this matter of taking the initiative of accepting and receiving purification from Him. It is as though He is saying, *'If you want to know how, watch Me."* As Jesus talks to the Father about us, He says, *"Father, for their sakes I sanctify Myself that they may be sanctified also, through the truth"* (John 17:19). Simply put, He is asking us to do the same thing that He, Himself is doing and has done for us.

A Clean Break With Sin

One of the best ways to make that 'clean break' with sin is to confess our sin. The last 5 verses of I John 1 start off with the word "if," which indicates that the statement is conditional. If we meet the conditions, the proposition of the preposition (if) is granted.

The condition before us is 'confession.'

"If we confess our sins, He is faithful and just to forgive us our sins, and to cleanse us from all unrighteousness." (I John 1:9)

This passage is directed to you, Christian, and not to some lost person. Second person plural pronouns are used in this verse alone, 5 different times. These type pronouns are used 19 times in those last 5 verses. Thus, the challenge and the responsibility to make a clean break with sin, and start the march toward holiness, is laid at our feet by the Word of God. Let's meet the conditions and start off with a clean slate. He will not only forgive the overt sins we have committed, but will cleanse us from all unrighteousness (innate sin).

STEP 2. Fill Your Mind With Good Things From The Word Of God

The great problem with many Christians is that their minds need to be renewed. Their minds are still cluttered, and are in disarray with the thoughts and intents of the old life. Therefore, they cannot think 'holy.' They cannot talk 'holy.' They cannot do 'holy.'

Remember, this is a purity and holiness of heart and life, and not merely an outward holiness. Outward holiness is the kind the Pharisees had. John Wesley called it *'Sour Holiness,'* and went a step further, and said, *"Sour holiness is the 'Devil's Religion'."*

Because this is a *'heart holiness'* it must begin in the heart and mind. The holiness of God starts, for the believer, in his heart and proceeds outward. Could that be what The Apostle Paul was trying to say to us when he wrote these words to the Church at Philippi? *"...Work out your own salvation with fear and trembling"* (Philippians 2:12). Again, we are looking at the solemn charge of respecting the Holiness of God. Whether we are working this heart holiness from the inside 'out,' or, whether we work at it every day, we are still dealing with the reputation of God. It can only be done one way, *"With fear and trembling."* This is serious. It is high time to stop playing around.

The 'Word of God' filling our minds is our very life. Jesus quoted the Old Testament and said, "Man shall not live by bread alone, but by every word that proceedeth out of the mouth of God" (Matthew 4:4). The Psalmist accredited the Word as being a cleansing factor in his life (Psalm 119:9).

Our Lord knew that we would need ammunition to keep up in our walk with Him. He gave us sufficient knowledge and mind renewing material to replace the things deposited in our minds by the world and Satan.

In order to truly get on the stretch for God in our ascent to holiness, we must re-program our computers. We need to get the world's garbage out of our minds and get the Word of God in. In the New Testament our Lord left us several itemized lists of Godly material with which to re-program our minds. These lists point out the real characteristics of *the Jesus-Kind of Christian.* Let's look at them and run a character check on Jesus, after which, we should factor these Christian graces into the fabric of our entire being.

Personal Computers

The hardware of your computer system is your *"Spirit, Soul, and Body."* The programs(software) you need to load into your *'very personal computer'* are listed below.

Program Number 1. The Beatitudes of Jesus. We will call them 'The Eight Progressive Steps to Sanctity' (Matthew 5:1 - 12). Steps: (1) Humility, (2) Penitence, (3) Meekness, (4) Spiritual Hunger, (5) Mercifulness, (6) Inward Purity, (7) Peacemaking, and (8) Sacrificial Suffering.

Program Number 2. Christian Love (Agape'). The Bible says that Love is the best gift and we can address it as 'The Primacy of Love *(Charity)'* (I Corinthians 13), because all other gifts are nothing without it. We will list these characteristics as 'The Marks of Love' Marks: (1) Patience, (2) Kindness, (3) Is not jealous, (4) Is not boastful, (5) Is not proud, (6) Is not rude, (7) Is not conceited, (8) Is not easily provoked, (9) Does not think evil, (10) Does not rejoice in evil, (11) Always: Protects, Trusts, Hopes, & Preserves, (12) Never fails. *"But now abide faith, hope, love, these three; but the greatest of these is love"* (1 Corinthians 13:13, NASB).

Program Number 3. The Fruit of the Spirit (Galatians 5:22 & 23). *The Fruit of the Spirit* is the Character of Jesus in you. A recreated human spirit can produce the following fruit: (1) Love, (2) Joy, (3) Peace, (4) Patience, (5) Kindness, (6) Goodness, (7) Faithfulness, (8) Gentleness, (9) Self-Control, *"And no law exists* *against any of these"(Galatians 5:23, Phillips). "...The fruit of the spirit is in all goodness, righteousness and truth; proving what is acceptable unto the Lord"* (Ephesians 5:9 & 10).

Program Number 4. Paul's "Food For Thought" (Philippians 4:8). Think on these things that are: (1) Truthful, (2) Honest/honorable, (3) Just/right, (4) Pure, (5) Lovely/attractive, (6) Excellent, (7) Praiseworthy. This 'Food for Thought' is a simple paragraph on mental health. These 'thoughts' are preceded in verse 7 by words concerning the *'Peace of God.'* This 'God Kind of Peace' passes all our understanding and it will keep our hearts and minds through Jesus Christ. Then in verse 8, the Apostle deals with the *'God of Peace.'* Here Paul admonishes us to *'Do'* what he has shown us. This will guarantee the Presence of the God of Peace. *To possess the peace of God, one must possess the God of peace.*

Program Number 5. The Garments of God's Elect (Colossians 3:12 - 14). These are *Christian Graces*, they are garments that we put on and wear. So, put on these clothes: (1) Compassion/ mercy, (2) Kindness, (3) Humility, (4) Gentleness\meekness, (5) Patience, (6) Endurance, (7) Forgiveness, (8) Love. "Above all things put on charity" (v. 14). *"...Adorn the doctrine of God our Savior in all things"* (Titus 2:10).

Program Number 6. The Ascending Steps of Christian Graces (II Peter 1:5 - 8). The Apostle Peter is sharing certain special steps toward Christian maturity and perfection. Before we list them we will allow the apostle to give us an introduction to this ascending scale of God's graces available to us. He says, *God's "divine power has granted to us everything pertaining to life and Godliness, through the true knowledge of Him who called us by His own glory and excellence (virtue). For by these He has granted to us His precious and magnificent promises, in order that by them you might become partakers of the divine nature, having escaped the corruption that is in the world by lust. Now for this very reason also, applying all diligence ..."* (verses 3 - 5b, NASB). Then, he gives us the steps He starts with (1) Faith, (2) Goodness, (3) Knowledge, (4) Self-Control, (5) Perseverance, (6) Godliness, (7) Brotherly Kindness, (8) Love (agape').

Program Number 7. Heavenly Wisdom (James 3:17 & 18, NEB). This wisdom from above is: (1) Pure; (2) Peace-loving, (3)

Considerate, (4) Open to reason, (5) Straight- forward, (6) Sincere, (7) Rich in Mercy and Kindly Deeds. This wisdom is full of spiritual fruit.

THE ABOVE ITEMS ON EACH LIST ARE GOOD, HOLY, WHOLESOME, AND COMPLIMENTARY THINGS HE HAS PLACED AT YOUR DISPOSAL TO LIVE BY. If you will practice getting rid of that old garbage from the world and reprogram your mind with these things, what else would there be for you to think about, talk about, or do? Having your mind loaded and charged with this kind of knowledge will make you wise as to the schemes and devices of Satan. Your mind supplied with this kind of knowledge and power will give you unprecedented strength in time of temptation. Be sure to keep the Truth (Word) active in your heart (John 15:3 & 17:17). God will use it to clean you up and make you holy. David knew exactly how to prevent sin from controlling his life. He hid God's word in his heart (Psalm 119:11). *"Thy word have I treasured in my heart, that I might not sin against thee"* (NASB).

STEP 3. Talk Right!

In order to live right (holy), bathe and baptize everything you do with sincere prayer. Among many of his other prayers, King David prayed to God and asked of Him…

> *"Let the words of my mouth and the meditation of my heart, be acceptable in thy sight, O lord, my strength, and my Redeemer."* (Psalm 19:14)

If you clean up your mind you can clean up your speech.

STEP 4. Do Right!

No doubt questions have been racing through your mind about lust and other such sins. Jesus addressed that situation and we alluded to it in Chapter 20 on, *"You Do Not Have To Compromise Your Integrity,"* as we dealt with inmate and overt sin. He gave us an itemized list of the sins of the heart, and told us that these sins are those that contaminate and defile us (Matthew 7:20-23).

From Contamination to Consecration

So it reverts back again to getting the garbage out of our minds, *"As a man thinks in his heart, so is he"* (Proverbs 23:7). If you truly desire to live a holy life, you must re-stock the warehouse of your mind with pure and wholesome material. Paul prayed for you that God would sanctify you completely (I Thess. 5:23). His special request in this prayer for you was that God would make you completely holy in spirit, soul, and body. Your mind is in your soul and it too can be sanctified. I think it is a great idea to pray for God to sanctify your mind.

Some of the right things that you can do to help you guard against sin are stated below:

Pray earnestly for God to continue to give you strength and deliverance in time of temptation (II Peter 2:9).

"...If you think you are standing firm, be careful that you don't fall! No temptation has seized you except what is common to man. And <u>God is faithful</u>, He will not let you be tempted beyond what you can bear. But when you are tempted, He will also provide a way out so that you can stand up under it." (1 Corinthians 10:13, NIV, *emphasis mine*).

Keep your mind on Jesus and His Word, especially His promises. There are nearly 9000 promises in the Bible and they were put there for you to utilize for your earth walk. Please reread II Corinthians 7:1 and II Peter 1:4 concerning God's promises. They will do great things for you if you utilize them.

Do spiritual warfare against the obstacles Satan might throw in your path.

"...I give unto you authority to tread upon serpents and scorpions, and over all the power of the enemy, and nothing shall injure you" Luke 10:19,NASB).

Put on the whole armor of God, that you may be able to stand, and having done all to stand (Ephesians 6:10 - 18). Your military issue as a soldier of Christ and His church is: (1) The belt of truth, (2) The breastplate of righteousness, (3)Combat Boots prepared for carrying the Gospel of Peace (See also Isa. 52:7), (4) The Shield of Faith, (5) The Helmet of Salvation, (6) The Sword of the Spirit (The Word of God),

Plus, *"Praying always with all prayer and supplication in the Spirit, and watching thereunto with all perseverance and supplication for all saints."* (Ephesians 6:18)

I have emphasized such all-inclusive words as: *'Always,'* and *'All.' What do such 'superlatives' mean in this setting (verse)?*

"...Thanks be to God, who always leads us in His triumph in Christ, and manifests through us the sweet aroma of the knowledge of Him in every place." (II Corinthians 2:14, NASB) "... Thanks be to God, Who giveth the victory through our Lord Jesus Christ." (I Corinthians 15:57)

I think it would be a great deal of help, at this point to pause and pray the words of this old hymn.

Whiter Than Snow

Lord Jesus, I long to be perfectly whole;

I want Thee forever to live in my soul;

Break down every idol, cast out every foe:

Now wash me, And I shall be whiter than snow.

Chorus:

Whiter than snow, yes, whiter than snow;

Now wash me, and I shall be whiter than snow.

Lord Jesus, look down from Thy throne in the skies

And help me to make a complete sacrifice;

I give of myself and whatever I know:

Now wash me, and I shall be whiter than snow.

Lord Jesus, for this I most humbly entreat;

I wait, Blessed Lord, at Thy crucified feet;

By faith, for my cleansing I see Thy blood flow:

Now wash me and I shall be whiter than snow.

— Nicholson and Fischer —

Continue to praise Him for the victory He continues to give you.

106

Appendix II

Why Holiness?

Why Am I So Sure and Positive about Holiness, Morality, Ethics and Integrity, whether it be Biblical, Ecclesiastical, or Personal? I am positive about holiness because the Bible is extremely positive about it.

Let's start at the beginning. Praise and glory be unto God, our Father because He has already blessed us with all spiritual blessings, in heavenly places, in Christ Jesus! In the same way He chose us in and through Jesus, "BEFORE THE FOUNDATION OF THE WORLD, that we should be holy and without blame," in His sight, in love" (Ephesians 1:3 & 4).

The Gospel of grace that I preach teaches us to live soberly, righteously, and godly in this present world Titus 2:11 & 12).

Jesus Himself left an example for us to follow in His footsteps (I Peter 2:21).

We are to purity ourselves, even as He is pure (I John 3:1 - 3).

Another apostle challenges us to purify ourselves, and, as we do, we are perfecting holiness, with a deep and an abiding respect for God. We can do this because we have scriptural promises to initiate and expedite it (II Corinthians 7:1).

We will stand, one day, before the judgment bar of God. God desires that His children be able to stand bold, without fear, and have freedom of speech as we present our case in the High Court of God. We can indeed, give a positive report about His life in us. "Herein is our love perfected," or 'this is the reason our love is made perfect' (I John 4:17), so we can have boldness and give a positive report. We will not have to bow our heads or apologize for living a Godly life. Why? "Because as He is so are we in this world." Read it for yourself!

God predestined and foreordained that we should be molded and conformed into the image of His Son, Jesus Christ (Romans 8:29). We are presently being transformed into the glorious image of Jesus Christ (II Corinthians 3:18).

Again, because of God's promises (see II Corinthians 7:1), we can become partakers (partners & sharers) of His divine nature (II Peter 1:4).

Prior to this, in verse 3, the apostle declares that God's power has (past tense) given us everything that pertains (requisite and suited) for life and Godliness.

Living this quality life brings us to higher altitudes to where we can get a clearer vision of God (Matthew 5:8 & Heb. 12:14). "They shall see God," or "without which no man shall see God." You can, no doubt, see Him here, on earth. Maybe you have wondered why?

If we exhibit 'The new man' we can experience a vision of our roots. We were originally created in the image of God (Genesis 1:26 - 27 and Ephesians 4:24). The 'new man' is created like God. Have you ever thought about this fact, we had original righteousness before we had original sin?

The life of holiness, purity, and integrity is one of the stipulations for serving God. This is to be done in His Holy Presence, all the days of our lives.

"...That we being delivered out of the hand of our enemies might serve Him without fear, In holiness and righteousness before Him, all the days of our life." (Luke 1:74 & 75)

In obedience, to the truth (see John 17:17 & 19) our hearts can be purified. And, because of that, we can love one another with a pure heart (I Peter 1:22). In the light of these verses, ask yourself this question: "What if we do not possess a pure heart or soul?"

Clean hands and a pure heart are two prime conditions for ascending the scale to the holy place (Psalm 24:3 - 4). We need to find (ascend to) the secret/holy place and dwell there.

One of the primary goals of our preaching and teaching (instruction or commandment) is to reap or receive love: out of a pure heart, a good conscience, and a sincere faith, for ourselves and our disciples (I Timothy 1:5).

Just as our earthly fathers disciplined and chastened us, God disciplines us so that we may share His holiness (Heb. 12:10).

We are in Christ and God has made Him to be our sanctification/holiness (I Corinthians 1:30). Jesus is indeed the Exalted Standard of Holiness.

Jesus died that you and I might become holy (Heb. 13:12).

We are admonished to discipline ourselves for the purpose of godliness (I Timothy 4:7 & 8).

Notice the profound, solid, and superlative nature of several words in I Thessalonians 5:23, such words as: Sanctify, wholly, whole, preserved blameless, How long? Unto the coming of our Lord Jesus Christ.

In warning us about the holocaust, terror, and the fury of destruction at the day of our Lord, Peter solemnly asks, "What manner of people ought we to be in holy conduct and godliness?" He adds, "Since you know this, be diligent to be found in Him in peace, spotless, and blameless" (II Peter 3:11 - 14).

In I Thessalonians 4:3, the Apostle Paul alerted us to this fact, to be holy is indeed to be in the will of God. Question: What if we are not holy?

Do you know that God has called you to holiness? Yes, read I Thessalonians 4:7, then 5:23 & 24. Paul says God is faithful to call you to holiness. We should be faithful to heed the call!

It is indeed a fact, God desires to establish our hearts unblamable in holiness (I Thess. 3:13).

Every individual needs to learn and know how to possess his vessel (body) in sanctification and honor (I Thess. 4:4). "Everyone of you should learn to control his body, keeping it pure and treating it with respect, and never allowing it to fall victim to lust, as do pagans with no knowledge of God." (Phillips)

If we are sanctified, Jesus is not ashamed to call us His brothers and sisters (Heb. 2:11).

The blood-bought and blood washed Christian Church is a holy family, kept by the Holy Father, redeemed by the Holy Son, and indwelt by the Holy Spirit.

To Sin Or Not To Sin That's The Question

Some people preach and teach that you can live above sin! Others, take an opposite view and proclaim, you can't help it, you have to sin. This is a battle that has been raging across the centuries. And I have no desire to get caught in the cross-fire. Some of the old preachers used to say, "Some people think the only way you can live above sin is to rent an apartment above a honky tonk."

Regardless of the stance you or I take, I am sure of this one thing, we can get by on much less sin than we are now experiencing, exercising and expediting. People in the church are grossly extravagant with sin. We have over spent our budget in this area. Just as the government makes budget cuts in different programs and services, the church needs to scale down and cut back in it's use of sin. In many cases the church places no restraints on sin. Government, business, and education do a much better job at policing their ranks than the church does. Sin is a luxury we simply cannot afford. In whatever area and to whatever degree, sin is the little fox that will spoil everything we do.

Appendix III
Questionable Questions?

No, questions that invoke positive answers!

Did Jesus die to take away our sins or not?

Will He take away our sins if we request it?

Did Jesus save us in our sins or from our sins?

Is He strong enough and pure enough to keep us clean, if we but ask Him (I John 1:7 & 9)?

Are our sins forgiven for our sakes or for His Name sake (I John 2: 12)?

Would you rather play than pray? If so, this lifestyle is not for you.

You profess the new birth, is it backed up by the new life?

Ponder this statement: "Praying men will stop sinning or sinning men will stop praying."[28]

Suggestion: Gather a group of Christians around you and discuss the scriptures listed in Appendix II. Glean from each verse and from each person involved, how to do a better job of keeping these little foxes from continually harassing you. To be in a group setting will help each one be accountable to each other.

Conclusion

I suppose you could say this book presents a call or a challenge to repentance, and therefore, to personal holiness and integrity. The things we have targeted in this little volume are personal character traits that can link one individual to another. One could easily say, these traits are either lines or gateways of communications between individuals, whether verbalized or not. These traits can either enhance or impede our social relationships. Some of these attributes really stand out, or, they are hidden or covered to prevent others from seeing them. Yet they are there, marking our relationships by, either prompting or restricting our associations. Since these are links or ties from one person to another, they become arteries or channels through which social contacts are made, and in some cases, maintained.

John Wesley said there is no holiness without social holiness. My interpretation of what Wesley meant was that Christians should be the catalysts in which the healing of our social ills are conceived, birthed, and nurtured. If we conceal our 'holiness,' in the sanctuary of our own hearts and never give it away, we are of all people most miserable. Thus, holy thoughts, attitudes, and spirits are not transferred. Other spirits and attitudes are being transferred, therefore there is no revival, only chaos, confusion, and disorder. But, we can make a difference, we can be the impetus and motivation for revival in our land. The healing of our land will definitely come about when the people who are called 'Christians,' humble themselves, and pray, seek God's face, and turn from or repent of their wicked ways (II Chronicles 7:14).

You say, "It's not that simple!" Yes, it really is 'that simple.' But what we actually need is a thorough cleansing of the Body of Christ, following the formula given in II Chronicles 7:14. Every Christian needs to learn humility and exhibit a servant's attitude in spirit, soul, and body. We need to repent individually, confess and worship collectively, and pray and progress unitedly to bring revival to our land.

Abraham sent his chief steward, Eliezer, to secure a bride for his son, Isaac. The steward was not to take a wife for Isaac from among the heathen daughters of the Canaanites. Abraham desired a chaste bride for his son. Eliezer was to go to the land of Abraham's people to accomplish his mission to receive a virgin bride for Abraham's son (Genesis 15:2 & Chapter 24).

In the same way, God the Father sent His Chief Agent, the Holy Spirit, into the world to secure a Bride for His Son, Jesus. This Bride is not to be found among the daughters of this world. She will not be any old gal off the streets, but will be a chaste Bride, blood-bought, without spot, or wrinkle, or any such thing. "...Christ loved the church, and gave Himself for it, that He might sanctify and cleanse it with the washing of water by the word, that He might present it to Himself a glorious church, not having spot, or wrinkle, or any such thing; but that it should be holy, and without blemish." (Ephesians 5:25b - 27)

Glory to God in the Highest! One day, some glorious day, Jesus will come for His chaste and virgin Bride and take Her away in His arms. He will then carry Her through the threshold of Heaven for an eternal and never ending honeymoon. Hallelujah! HALLELUJAH!

THE MISSION OF
INTERNATIONAL GOSPEL OUTREACH

"IGO" is an interdenominational missionary servicing agency whose mission is:

"To influence the world by serving the church worldwide.

We do this by

educating, equipping and employing World Christians

to become

Pray-ers, Do-ers, Send-ers and Go-ers."

Any questions concerning the book The Little Foxes by Bertist Rouse or the missionary outreaches of "IGO" can be answered by contacting the office. Return the form below or phone/fax.

Name:_____

Address:_____

City:_____State:_____Zip Code_____

Phone(s) Home:_____Work:_____

IGO
P.O. Box 1008, Semmes, AL 36575-1008 USA
Phone (251) 645-2117 Fax (251) 645-2118

www.igoministries.org

Endnotes

[1] Charles F. Pfeiffer & Everett F. Harrison, The Wycliffe Bible Commentary (Nashville, Tennessee: The Southwestern Company, 1962), 598

[2] Stuart B. Flexner, ed., "Reader's Digest Family Word Finder" (Pleasantville, NY: The Reader's Digest Association, 1990).

[3] William Morris, ed., The American Heritage Dictionary of The English Language (Boston: The Houghton Mifflin co., 1976).

[4] Bill Gothard, Research In Principles of Life, Basic Seminar Textbook, (Oak Brook, IL: Institute of Basic Life Principles, 1981) 18.

[5] Oswald Chambers, My Utmost For His Highest (New York: Dodd, Meade & Co. 1935) 146

[6] Chambers, 272

[7] E. Arden Almquist, "Debtor Unashamed: The Road To Mission Is A Two-Way Street," (Chicago, Illinois: Covenant Publications, 1993), 39.

[8] Gothard, 18.

[9] Gothard, 101

[10] Mabel Williamson, "Have We No Rights" (Chicago: Moody Press, 1957), 9.

[11] Gothard, 80

[12] Mrs. Charles E. Cowan, "Springs In The Valley" (Grand Rapids: Zondervan, 1977), 23.

[13] Chambers, 182.

[14] W. E. Vine, "An Expository Dictionary of New Testament Words" (Westwood, N J: Fleming H. Revell Co., 1966), 129

[15] Vine, 286

[16] Vine, 173.

[17] Vine, 280

[18] Harrison, 1324 & 1325

[19] Marvin R. Vincent, "Word Studies In The New Testament." Vol. IV (Peabody, Mass.: Hindrickson Publishers), 548

[20] Vine, 170

[21] Vine, 107

[22] Porter Barrington, The Christian Life New Testament (Nashville, Tennessee: Thomas Nelson, Inc., 1978), 435

[23] Merril F. Unger & William White, Jr., Nelson's Expository Dictionary of the Old Testament (Nashville, Tennessee: Thomas Nelson Publishers, 1980), 379 & 381

[24] Oswald Chambers, "Still Higher For His Highest" (Grand Rapids, Michigan: Zondervan Publishing House, 1977), 174

[25] K. E W. Prior. "Decision Magazine," (Minneapolis, MN: Billy Graham Evangelistic Association). October '93, Vol. 34,No. 10,p. 25 & 26.

[26] Vine, 225

[27] Harrison, 1273

[28] This quote, by Leonard Ravenhill, I pull from my memory, not having a literary or written reference.

Made in the USA
Coppell, TX
31 October 2021